PARIS
UNDER
THE
OCCUPATION

PARIS UNDER THE OCCUPATION

by
GÉRARD WALTER

Translated from the French by
TONY WHITE

THE ORION PRESS
New York

First Printing

as La vie á Paris sous L'occupation
Library of Congress Catalog Card Number: 60–13616
Designed by Wladislaw Finne
Manufactured in the United States of America

FOREWORD

The aim of this book is to evoke certain aspects of life in Paris during the German occupation, as seen through the eyes of certain Parisian newspapers of the period.

I say "certain aspects," because this book does not claim to cover everything. The aspects it deals with are strictly limited, and have been determined by considerations of quality rather than quantity. It is preferable, I believe, that the reader should know this from the start.

I have said, also, "certain Parisian newspapers." This means that I have used only publications of a specific kind —publications that are commonly grouped under the somewhat inadequate heading of "German newspapers written in French." I should point out, however, that in putting together this book my role has merely been that of a compiler. What I have done is to select from a number of Parisian newspapers, published during the years 1940–1944, various passages that characterize the period. My aim has been to build up a documentary record which, although it is unavoidably one-sided and needs to be read against a similar record compiled from the Resistance press, may still prove to be a useful contribution toward understanding the dual problem (applying equally to both soldiers and civilians) raised by the last war. That is the problem of determining how the population of an occupied capital city was treated, and how that same population reacted when its moral and practical conventions underwent a swift and radical transformation.

Let me explain. During the course of the Second World War, Nazi Germany managed to subdue eight European capitals by force of arms. The administrative machinery set up to deal with them was generally uniform, and—national differences aside—was applied in equal measure to French and Norwegians, Poles and Belgians, Greeks and Dutch, among others.

The general principle and starting point was everywhere the same: Since the National-Socialist regime was best suited to the real needs and spiritual aspirations of modern Europe, defeated peoples had to be convinced of the regime's superiority, and alienated from their own governments, which were guilty of having opposed it. This was to be achieved by every possible means: persuasion, force, corruption and so on. The press was to be the chief weapon in the arsenal of psychological warfare. In any event, it was the one that was most subtly handled, especially in Paris.

In capitals such as Brussels, Warsaw, Oslo and Athens, the normal dose of propaganda—according to Dr. Goebbels' proficient services—from half a dozen controlled and conformist periodicals, could be injected into the patient's body without causing unpleasant disturbances. But its application, pure and simple, to the capital of France proved both insufficient and, in practice, impossible. The formula had to be made more supple, more flexible.

The German propaganda experts quickly learned their lessons and began to use tactics of some subtlety. These consisted of exploiting the long-standing and intimate link between the Parisian and *his* newspaper. They realized it was essential to respect the "style" of the Paris press. They instructed their French employees to produce newspapers closely modeled on the ones that Parisians had always favored. There was to be nothing in their pages that would shock their readers' habits, and the items they were accustomed to were not to be omitted. So that while the Déats, the Luchaires and the Suarez strove to fulfill their appointed tasks on the front page, the other pages were devoted to various "world reports," short stories, historical and strictly non-political narratives, and literary, dramatic and art criticism. Music, the movies, radio, and above all sports, played a large part, as did the hundred and one problems of everyday life. In these areas, journalists were free to indulge their critical judgments as long as the German authorities were not involved. The result was that what they lost on the merry-go-rounds, they regained on the swings—all the more so, because the Germans themselves openly encouraged press campaigns, and sometimes even went so far as to play the role of peacemakers called in to correct the excesses and failures of the French authorities. It is obvious, therefore, that, allowing for their political slant, the "occupied" newspapers provide a wealth of information and throw considerable light on conditions of life in occupied Paris.

This "occupied" press (I ask the reader's permission to use, if not abuse, this handy abbreviation) is a social and psychological (I almost wrote "pathological") phenomenon that deserves careful study. No work has yet been devoted to it, except Jean Quéval's, which is, in any case, unfinished (see the Bibliography, p. 209). It remains obscured under a thick veil of silence and embarrassment that increases with the years. Granted that this collection of muck makes the gorge rise, but surely the historian should, to quote the memorable words of Pierre Caron, *"avoir l'odorat solide"** (*Massacres de Septembre,* p. VI). Personally, I have never believed that history should be written with kid gloves. But that is no reason for not writing it at all. The Paris press being what it is, it follows that its history could not have been other than what it was. It would falsify the perspective to omit from consideration a period in which there were active more than fifty publications with a total daily circulation of three million, (the number refers to Paris newspapers only, and omits weeklies), and which involved about a thousand collaborators (using that word in its professional sense).

G. W.

* Literally: "to have a staunch nose." That is, to have an iron stomach, or strong palate.

CONTENTS

ILLUSTRATIONS

Following page

PARIS
UNDER
THE
OCCUPATION

PARISIENS,
Soyez prudents
Conformez-vous
aux instructions données

5c 50

Le Matin

5c 50

PARISIENS,
N'écoutez pas
Ne suivez pas
les conseils des autres

37e ANNÉE — N° 20.534 — EDITION DE PARIS — LUNDI 17 JUIN 1940

A nos lecteurs

A la demande de M. Villey, préfet de la Seine jointe à celle de M. Langeron préfet de police,

Le Matin reparaît à Paris.

La vie continue.

L'œuvre d'un journal est d'éclairer l'opinion publique. Son devoir est de le faire dans la recherche de la vérité.

Le gouvernement ayant cru devoir quitter la capitale, a emmené avec lui tous les journaux, leurs rédacteurs, le personnel technique, enfin tous les éléments nécessaires pour faire une feuille d'information.

Aussi le public excusera le Matin de l'insuffisance de ses informations et la qualité de sa production.

Mais les préfets, seuls représentants du gouvernement de la République, se sont adressés au Matin pour que la population parisienne ait un journal.

C'est donc avec l'amour du devoir que rédacteurs, compositeurs, clicheurs, vendeurs se sont groupés hier autour de leur maison et que nous paraissons.

« LE MATIN ».

POUR AVOIR du lait condensé de la viande fraîche de la viande congelée et de la farine

PEUPLE DE PARIS

Les troupes allemandes ont occupé Paris.

La ville est placée sous le gouvernement militaire.

LE COMMANDANT EN CHEF DU GROUPE D'ARMÉES.

La circulation dans les rues de Paris

à partir de 21 heures

Pour trouver du travail

Paris sera ravitaillé

Réquisition des boulangers

des restaurateurs

et des commerçants détaillants en alimentation

Constitution d'un corps sanitaire pour le service soc[illegible]

UN CONSEIL DE DÉFENSE NATIONALE s'est réuni hier et a délibéré sur la réponse du président Roosevelt

UN APPEL du préfet de la Seine à la population parisienne

Aux commerçants et aux Parisiens

AUTORISATION D'AVANCES aux receveurs-percepteurs

Aux Halles et dans les marchés

Paris est propre

Des écoles de Paris et de la banlieue sont rouvertes

LES SESSIONS DU CONSEIL MUNICIPAL ET DU CONSEIL GÉNÉRAL AJOURNÉES A QUAND ?

PRENEZ GARDE AUX CHIENS ABANDONNÉS

Les tirages d'emprunt sont suspendus

La préfecture de la Seine veut éviter le chômage...

AVIS ET COMMUNIQUÉS

Le « MATIN » paraît à Paris et en Province aujourd'hui

LES ENFANTS les vieillards et les rentiers évacués en province ne sont pas oubliés

Une délégation municipale à l'Hôtel-de-Ville

La circulation du Métropolitain

Tout stock de denrées repéré sera réquisitionné et mis en vente

Les traitements des instituteurs et institutrices de Paris

Une délégation spéciale est instituée à Puteaux

Les affiches officielles

LE COMMUNIQUÉ OFFICIEL ALLEMAND publié par ordre DE L'AUTORITÉ MILITAIRE ALLEMANDE

"Le Matin," June 17, 1940: birth of the "occupied" press.

Germans on the Quai D'Orsay.

THE EXODUS

Paris threatened

On June 6, the Somme front broke. The following day, the Aisne positions were crumbling. The Germans began to penetrate the Paris defense line, and an enveloping movement threatened from the east and west. Chaotic swarms of disbanded soldiers fled toward the capital.

Colonel Groussard, who had arrived the previous day from Alsace to take over his duties as Chief-of-Staff, Paris region, recalled in his *Memoirs:*

"Camps to receive them were quickly improvised at Colombes, Maisons-Laffitte and Massy-Palaiseau . . . Within three days, they were inundated. A serious problem then arose: because of the shortage of cadres, and the poverty of their equipment, these soldiers could not be sent back to the front. The absence of trains and trucks meant they could not be removed to the interior. Furthermore, after witnessing over a period of several appalling days the hopeless disparity between the enemy's strength and their own, their morale was far from reassuring. All of them were to some extent the prey of disillusion, despair and anxiety, and they only succeeded in making each other more fearful. Units were mixed together, which meant that discipline was relaxed—in fact, hardly existed. This vast horde, which, for the most part, had no hand in its own downfall, could not under any circumstances be allowed to enter Paris. Its presence there would undoubtedly have led to disastrous consequences. That was why, on the evening of the twelfth, we decided to evacuate all fugitives to positions in the rear by road, as far as possible assigning them cadres. Until then, it had often been difficult to control these troops, who, on the whole, made no secret of their aversion to the idea of returning to the fighting under such atrocious conditions."[1]

There were also daily arrivals of laborers, recruited by the civilian authorities at the rate of three thousand men a day. A defense plan for the capital had been drawn up at the very beginning of the war. It envisaged a work program of considerable size, requiring a vast amount of manual labor. As Colonel Groussard wrote:

"It would have been advisable to put this program into action during the autumn and winter of 1939–1940. But the High Command issued orders for its execution only when it was obvious that the Somme and Aisne positions could no longer withstand the enemy thrust. Besides, in the atmosphere of haste and anxiety, the civilian laborers, once arrived, were organized, distributed and assigned in a completely improvised manner. All this took place in a context of chaos and panic. As it turned out, the workers were of no use whatsoever, and, wherever they were, only complicated the task of the fighting units."

July 4, 1940

Evacuation of the press

The government decided to leave Paris on the afternoon of the ninth of June.

M. Jean Prouvost, Minister of Information, and owner-director of *Paris-Soir,* was at that time in his office at the Hôtel Continental. He was receiving a delegation of American journalists, who had come, toward the end of the afternoon, to acquaint him with their worries and difficulties. The minister reassured them:

"Whatever happens, the government will not leave Paris. You stay with us. If there's anything you want to know, come and see me—tomorrow, the next day, whenever you like; you'll always find me."[2]

The Americans left, their anxiety eased. They had hardly left when a phone call informed the minister that the government would be leaving the same night, and instructed him to start evacuating his staff.

There was a knock on the door. It was Pierre Lazareff. He, too, had come for instructions, and wanted to know what was going on. In his own words:

"In the huge room where he had his office, Jean Prouvost was sitting alone, frowning, the pallor of his face emphasized by the harsh glare of the electric light.

" 'Is the government staying, or going?'. . . .

"Whenever he was under emotional stress, Jean Prouvost used to twiddle his small, fair mustache.

" 'We're leaving immediately.'

" 'Where are we going? To Tours?'

" 'Yes.'

" 'What about the press?'

" 'They'll have to stay here as long as possible. But keep as few people as you can at *Paris-Soir*. Evacuate the others as best you can.'

"The door opened, and Jean Fayard, the minister's private secretary, came in, wearing a smart captain's uniform.

" 'Good afternoon, folks,' he said, smiling, as if we were sitting over a cup of tea. Then he turned to Jean Prouvost, and went on:

" 'It's most infuriating. In spite of what you said earlier, the heads of its newspapers refuse to continue publishing in Paris. They say it's their duty to follow the government.'

" 'Do they know we're leaving?'

" 'Of course. And they also say they've no further sources of information. So they're packing up.'

" 'All of them?'

" 'All of them.'

" 'If it's all right by you,' I said, 'we'll stay till the Germans reach the porte de la Chapelle.'

" 'Very well. But don't do anything rash.' "

Lazareff hurried back to the rue du Louvre, and began to organize—or, as he put it, "improvise is the better word"—the evacuation of his paper. He had decided to go to Clermont-Ferrand. As he wrote:

"Pierre Laval, always a good businessman, offered us lodgings, provided we used the printing press of his paper, *Le Moniteur.* We knew he had broad-mindedly offered his services to almost every paper, from the Socialist *Populaire* to the royalist *Action Française.* We were the first to hire the press and the rooms. But the facilities were hopelessly inadequate. There were 150 beds for 800 people. And then everyone insisted on transporting and lodging his family, as well as himself. . . ."

The evacuation took the whole of June 10. As Lazareff wrote:

"At midnight, all that was left was a rear-guard of volunteers: a dozen linotypists, sleeping by their machines, a dozen rotary press operators and lithographers unashamedly camping out in the empty directorial offices, a handful of newsdealers and newsboys comfortably settled on the chutes off which they normally snatched the bundles of papers as they came fresh from the printing presses. . . ."

But he was surprised to see a large group of unfamiliar and unexpected colleagues installed in the editorial offices. As he wrote:

"Official censors had also settled in at *Paris-Soir,* because it was then the only newspaper still being printed in Paris. They had their camp beds with them, and meals were being brought them from the bistro on the corner. Their chief, a major nicknamed *Trompe-la-Mort,** a hero of the First World War, was a humorist from the Midi. He told me, in his indescribable accent:

" 'Most of those I picked to stay with me are absolutely furious with you. You see, they gave me all the rich men's sons, the ones who know how to pull strings, the boys with friends in high places. They thought they were sitting pretty at the censorship office, with no danger of getting mixed up in the fighting. And now their colleagues have gone off to Tours, and they've got to stay here, just because *Paris-Soir* wants to call attention to itself and go on appearing. And the Germans could turn up any minute! I'm the only one who sees the funny side of it.'

"As it turned out, those censors were the most obliging workers we ever had. None of them bothered to cut or shorten any of the articles. . . . They even helped us to edit the dispatches so the paper could come out earlier, and spent the rest of the time persuading us that we were mad to sit there writing on top of a volcano."

At two o'clock in the afternoon, the paper came off the presses. The crowd that had gathered opposite the block fought for copies. Lazareff, who was watching from his office, noted:

"What struck me was that only those who were staying were interested in the news. Not one of the crowd that was leaving so much as stuck out a hand to any of our newsboys; they had settled for a long journey, and their one thought was to get away."

At three o'clock, an intelligence officer arrived from the Paris military government. Lazareff saw bad

* Literally: "death cheater, or dicer with death."

news written all over his face. He took him into his office. Major Paleirac followed them in. The officer told them:

"I think you'd better go. The situation's pretty chaotic. . . . If the Germans break through anywhere with their tanks, it'll be over quickly."

"And what about the defense of Paris from inside?"

The officer gestured eloquently. There was a long silence. Major Paleirac whistled through his teeth:

"That's it, then!"

"All right," I said, as soon as I got my breath back, "we'll go. . . ."

The departure

From the rue du Louvre we pass to the Invalides, and Colonel Groussard:

"The sudden evacuation of the ministries, without any warning, during the night of June 9 and 10, only made the position worse. Every means of transport—trucks and cars—vanished in the twinkling of an eye. In fact, the civilian authorities requisitioned everything they could lay their hands on, without the slightest regard for military necessities. Also, the population soon learned of the government's decision, and hurried after their leaders by every available means. Until then, many had hesitated, but now they turned their faces to the south and made off . . .

"The unexpected flight of the government triggered off a state of affairs disastrous to Parisians, who were now left without orders or advice. The entire population—to the eternal disgrace of the country's leaders—was stricken with panic. In their alarm and confusion, these leaders had been guilty of appalling negligence. For instance, on the evening of the eleventh, General Dénain informed me that the Ministry of War had failed to make any arrangements to evacuate the Franco-Polish mission. After the utmost difficulty, I sent them six busses. The same day, there was a call from General Mariaux to say he had no instructions for evacuating the Musée de l'Armée. I dug up a couple of trucks which I handed over to him so he could evacuate the most precious objects from the museum. . . ."[3]

Professor André Morize, deputy commissioner to the Ministry of Information, recorded:

"Up to the last moment, I had no idea if I was supposed to go to Moulins, as ordered, or to Tours. The departure hour of my train was changed four times, and the station twice."[4]

There were also tens of thousands of exempted specialists in the factories and workshops of the neighboring suburbs. No one knew what to do with them. As Colonel Groussard wrote:

"Orders and counterorders followed each other so vigorously and rapidly, that those in charge almost seemed to be getting some kind of malign pleasure from their cruel sport. Some of these wretched workers ended up, hopeless and starving, in crowded railroad stations; others were left to tramp the roads in pathetic, disorganized columns, and I only wish I knew who the idiot was that collected about a hundred of these poor devils, advised them to make for the south as fast as they could on foot, and gave them Marseilles as a rallying point!"[5]

In trying to describe what was happening in the streets a distinction must be made. Only the main arteries of the exodus, leading to the porte d'Orléans and the porte d'Italie, presented the Dantesque spectacle so often depicted. It lasted three days: the eleventh, twelfth and thirteenth of June. No attempt will be made here to study the alarm that affected Paris as a whole. As a psychological curiosity, it resembled the Great Fear of August-September, 1789, which ravaged the towns and countryside of France in the early days of the Revolution.

A Swiss journalist, whose nationality guaranteed him complete immunity, later asked himself why he had left Paris. Obviously puzzled, and searching for a reason, he wrote:

"I left Paris because it suddenly changed in appearance, because I was living opposite the Ministry of the Interior, and there was a long convoy of military trucks parked outside, and M. Mandel's dossiers were piling up on them.

"I left Paris, because the stores and offices were closing, because telephones were working only in the central Paris area, because transportation was getting scarce, because the streets seemed a little emptier each day, and everything that goes to make up a street and gives it its confidence, was disappearing. It's amazing what the street cleaner and the newsboy do for the look of a place. The day the street cleaner fails to turn up and the paper stand stays shut, the street begins to panic. . . . On Wednesday, June 12, at 6 P.M., a herd of cows from the Ferme d'Auteuil was wandering freely in the place de l'Alma, with no one to look after it. The creatures were hungry and their bellowings echoed sadly in the deserted quays. Occasional passers-by scarcely bothered to turn and look at this astonishing sight. It was probably after witnessing this spectacle that I decided to leave Paris."[6]

A number of writers, overanxious to stir their readers' imaginations, described the city as a "necropolis"; this impression, however, is contradicted by various eyewitness accounts.

For instance, Professor André Morize, who arrived in the United States after many hardships, gave this picture (in the book previously cited), which remained fixed in his memory:

"Crossing Paris, to leave by the porte d'Italie, I followed the quays along the Seine, and had a farewell glimpse of that delightful prospect of water and greenery. While the city was enjoying its last moments of liberty, the booksellers had opened their stalls and were waiting for customers. Opposite the Institut, a storekeeper was dusting over his medals and knickknacks."

Léon Blum, who returned to Paris on the eleventh with Marx Dormoy, wrote in his memoirs:

"Marx Dormoy left me to go up to Belleville, above the Père Lachaise cemetery. When he returned, he was still amazed by the immense contrast he had seen. Belleville, a working-class area, was full of life and animation, and carrying on normally, as if it were part of another world altogether."

During all this time, to quote André Morize:

". . . mangling the torn and anguished body of France, entering her from all sides, ravaging her horribly with fire and sword, everywhere spreading its tentacles; fighting for her roads, severing her escape routes with cold steel, the other army, bent on her destruction, marched inexorably onwards.

"A huge army, almost untouched, a cruel machine in perfect condition, organized, disciplined, all-powerful, with a vast supply of superb equipment, and men that were part of it. Men on trucks, on motorbikes, on bridges hastily flung across rivers where heroes made desperate last stands, were continually advancing, grenades, rifles, revolvers in hand, machine-like men, steeped in discipline and fanatical loyalty to their leaders. Thousands of them, more and more, driving their murderous blades from all sides into the heart of France, hacking their way through the massive legions of the defeated—the conquering flood!"

THE GERMANS ENTER PARIS

Paris, an open city

On June 10, a group of city councilors went to ask Paul Reynaud: "Is Paris to be defended?" The President of the Council passed along their question to General Weygand. The Commander-in-Chief replied:

"The city of Paris is an open city, but it is situated in the center of a large military zone, with its front about thirty kilometers from the capital. In order to preserve Paris' identity as an open city, my aim is to avoid defending the city along its perimeter of old walls and forts."[8]

By that time, the Germans had crossed the Seine to the west of Paris and, in the east, their armored cars had reached Château-Thierry.

The next day, June 11, General Weygand sent all his army commanders an order marked "Secret and Personal":

"In view of the present state of the fighting, the possibility must be considered . . . of the Basse-Seine, Paris defense position, Marne front being broken. In this eventuality, it is the wish of the Commander-in-Chief to protect the heart of the country as long as possible, and maintain the greatest possible number of large units."

It was, in fact, a warning order for a general withdrawal of the French army to the Caen-Tours-Dijon-Dôle line, which General Weygand proposed to set up when he could no longer envisage the possibility of any coördinated defense system.

In Paris itself, on June 10, General Héring, the military governor, took over command of an army. On the eleventh, he was still convinced the capital would be defended. He summoned the two prefects to tell them: "We're holding on! No question of evacuating without government orders."

He sent General Lannurien to general headquarters for instructions. General Weygand's reply was:

"General Héring will take control of the Paris army, and will remain with it to the end. General Dentz, to whom he will hand over his duties as governor, is to remain on the spot until and when, should the case arise, the Germans enter the city." Paris would be declared an open city, "therefore, neither the perimeter of old forts, nor the line of old ramparts will be defended; nothing will be destroyed, retreating troops will bypass the city, and so avoid crossing it."

The meeting took place in a park. In a nearby avenue, Paul Reynaud and Marshal Pétain were strolling about waiting for Sir Winston Churchill to arrive. The Commander-in-Chief went up to them, and informed them with regard to his decision about Paris. Neither raised any objection. Afterwards, at Pétain's trial, General Weygand said: "I took it on myself to declare Paris an open city. I took the initiative, and the entire responsibility is mine."

This was on the eleventh, toward the end of the afternoon. The next day, the twelfth, General Weygand confirmed his decision by phone to General Héring. The same day, a powerful thrust brought the Germans to Évreux in the west, and Montreuil in the east. At 1 P.M., Weygand ordered a general retreat. The "Paris defense position" was abandoned during the night of the twelfth to thirteenth. On the morning of the thirteenth, Héring effected a withdrawal which brought his army front to the rear of Paris, on the line Rambouillet-Juvisy. He left the Invalides, and transferring his headquarters to Soizy, left Dentz the task of receiving the Germans who, by the end of the afternoon, had reached Aubervilliers and Bondy. These units consisted of armored cars of the Silesian Division, Tenth Army, part of Von Bock's Army Group. That evening, General von Küchler, commanding the Tenth Army, announced by radio that he was sending a delegate to Saint-Denis. The message was picked up by a city-police radio station and immediately transmitted to the Invalides. General Dentz was of two minds. He telephoned general headquarters. In his opinion, the commander of an open city was not empowered to negotiate with the enemy. General headquarters not only confirmed Dentz' opinion, but also agreed that General Héring had no authority to receive a delegate. Thus, seeing it was pointless to inform him, Dentz decided to let the German offer drop, and did not reply to the message. As Colonel Groussard later wrote:

"We considered that military commanders left in an open city by a belligerent state were solely responsible for maintaining order until the enemy's arrival, and not for parleying with him."[9]

At the Invalides, it was still not yet known that things had gone badly at Saint-Denis. The German delegate's car had been greeted with machine-gun bullets, and the officer killed. His second-in-command turned back and hurriedly regained the German lines.

It seems that when General von Küchler learned that his delegate had been killed, he became violently angry and wanted to order an immediate bombardment of the capital. But he let himself be persuaded by his Chief-of-Staff, General Marx, and at 2:25 A.M. a new message was sent out: "German delegate killed. Seek murderer. Delegates till 5 A.M. German time on the fourteenth, at Sarcelles. Comply—otherwise attack ordered on Paris."[10] This time Dentz replied that he would send two of his officers.

The Germans arrive

Major Devouges and Lieutenant Holtzer arrived at Sarcelles at five in the morning. There they found a German captain who had been waiting an hour for them at the town hall, because the French officers had not allowed for the difference between French and German time. They were taken to Écouen, where they were met by a staff officer of the Tenth Army, Major Brink, who informed them that the German army wanted to pass through the capital without use of force. This was dependent on four conditions:
1. That all resistance would cease on the Saint-Germain-Versailles-Meaux front.
2. That order would be guaranteed in Paris and the suburbs.
3. That public services would continue to function (water, gas, electricity).
4. That the entire population would remain at home for a period of forty-eight hours.
Major Devouges observed that point 3 contradicted point 4, so Brink waived it and the affair was settled.

No sooner had negotiations ended (it was then

5:30 A.M.) when police headquarters was notified that two truckloads of German troops and five or six motorcyclists had passed through the porte de la Villette. At 5:35 A.M., German troops could be seen in the rue de Flandre, moving in the direction of the Gare du Nord and the Gare de l'Est. Toward 6:30 A.M., a motorized column could be seen passing the Invalides on its way to Neuilly. As the advance continued, traffic police peeled off and stationed themselves at different points along the route. Only an hour later, the French delegates could be seen returning to the Invalides to announce that agreement had been reached. Meanwhile, other troops had made their way towards the Étoile. At 7:30 A.M., some cars pulled up outside the Hôtel Crillon. A general stepped out of one of them, followed by several officers. It was General von Stutnitz, who had been appointed military commander of Paris. His staff installed itself in the lobby of the hotel. His first action was to send one of his aides to the Invalides to claim the restitution of German flags that had been surrendered after the previous war. Dentz, whose first contact this was with the enemy authorities, replied that he did not know where they were. If the Germans wanted them badly enough, they could come and look for them, and take them away themselves. His reply met with little or no objection.

Meanwhile, German units were flowing toward the esplanade from the right bank, both along the quays, and across the Pont Alexandre III. One after another, infantrymen, artillerymen with their guns, and light tanks crossed the entrance, and pulled up at the different buildings as if they were moving into familiar billets. There was no jostling, no hesitation; officers were posted here and there, orders in one hand and signaling with the other. The whole operation was punctuated by short, guttural words of command.

Reaction of the people

How did the population react? Colonel Groussard answered the question categorically:

"The agony of Paris passed off in a state of calm. The civilian population made no attempt to react. It did nothing at all. It was apathetic. Parisians—at least, those who were left—showed complete indifference."

And he went on:

"One of our officers who was at police headquarters when the German troops arrived, came back to the Invalides . . . and gave us our first impressions of how the population had reacted. . . .

"From Belleville to Pigalle, from Menilmontant to the Champs-Élysées, officers and men of the German forces were everywhere ceaselessly accosted by passers-by of all classes, who joked with the enemy, and offered them any kind of help they wanted."[11]

This cut-and-dried version can, however, be slightly qualified by referring to one or two civilian accounts.

For instance, this unnamed woman, wife of an ordinary civil servant living in the fourteenth *arrondissement,* wrote:

"Saw the first Germans passing down the avenue du Maine, artillery, infantry, supply columns of chestnut horses with bleached tails, and green, canvas-topped wagons.

"I collapsed on a bench, weeping.

"A woman spectator, her face tense and unmoved, spoke to me: 'You mustn't cry like that, dear; you'll only encourage them.' "

LA RÉVOLUTION NATIONALE,
November 9, 1941

This testimony is the more convincing because it was published at the height of the occupation in one of the "occupied" newspapers most loyal to the "cause of collaboration," and, at the time, the woman had nothing to gain by it.

Here is another. This time from a metalworker, probably one of the unfortunate specially exempt workers mentioned earlier in answer to a question asked by the weekly, *La Gerbe:*

"I was in Paris on June 14. What were my feelings? I shall never forget them. I took my bike and thought of going for a ride. I went around the eighth and sixth *arrondissements,* the city center, the ninth and tenth, and part of the suburbs. Well, this is how it was: in the well-to-do areas—nothing, not a soul; all the windows were bolted. In the the working-class areas, people everywhere. . . .

"By midday, they were fraternizing with the Germans. Some were even going a bit far. In the rue Lafayette, as they went by, there was a large woman jumping up and down. She kept on repeating: 'Aren't they handsome? Look at the horses! No food for ten years? Just look at those handsome men! And the guns! And motorbikes! So they've got no gasoline, eh? And no equipment? We've been well had!'

"Finally, I saw she was going to cheer. I felt I had to say something:

" 'Hey, take it easy, old girl, what about our boys who died?' "

July 11, 1940

The enthusiasm and admiration shown by this woman, which was no doubt what persuaded *La Gerbe* to print this impression, shows, as through a magnifying glass, the state of mind of the working-class Parisian, and his strong sense of having been despicably betrayed. He gaped incredulously at the well-dressed, well-shod troops, because for months and months the papers had claimed that the German soldiers had nothing but rags to their backs, and were short of everything. In the working-class areas, housewives almost swooned to see mobile canteens doling out portions of boiled beef and potatoes that would have done a whole family proud, because up to the very last, the same papers had dinned into their ears tales of "fish-less fish paste" and "eggless omelettes," on which the Germans were supposed to be existing. It is practically certain that if there had not been such a striking contrast between the lies served up to the Parisians and the reality that suddenly faced them, they would have experienced, from the very beginning, a natural hostility to the invader. In fact, their admiration for their conquerors was a bitter expression of the disgust they felt for their own leaders. And the apathy, which Colonel Groussard condemned, simply mirrored their fierce repudiation of a corrupt regime, a repudiation which, less than two years later, turned to violent nostalgia.

A woman living in the fourteenth *arrondissement* went to queue up at a Prisunic where apparently "out of eighty salespeople, only four had stayed." As she waited, she listened to what was being said around her:

"People are talking. What strikes them is:

"1. The German soldiers are well equipped. Some women have nervously fingered their field-gray uniforms. They say it's real wool.

"2. They have been fighting, and yet they're clean-shaven and better turned out than the French soldiers who came through Paris from the fighting.

"3. Their manners are good. They ask for things and pay for them with German marks. Nobody knows what the mark is worth; so they're probably getting fantastic bargains, but they have good manners!

"4. The people are resentful: they keep mentioning treason and betrayal."

LA GERBE,
July 11, 1940

Meanwhile, an unimportant but typical incident took place. The customers were called in one by one by an old doorkeeper. She said:

"When it came to my turn, a feldwebel and two soldiers came straight in instead of joining the queue. I stopped the feldwebel and motioned to him to join the line; he agreed good-naturedly, but the old porter said to me gloomily: 'Let them in first, madame; they're the conquerors,' and he called them back in again."

LA GERBE,
July 11, 1940

In some places, people stared at the Germans as if they were strange beasts, and were to be feared. A woman from Neuilly noted:

"On the Pont de Neuilly, a sanitary detachment halted along the side of the road. The men were grimed with dust and sweat, and their faces drawn with fatigue. It was 11 A.M. They had been waiting there three hours, watching the local people, but not daring to ask for a cup of coffee or if they might go into one of the yards and wash their hands. People stood around, a few yards off, watching them, with no sign of hatred, but still rather nervous. They would have liked to talk to them, find out where they came from, how the French army was getting on, but they didn't dare. They walked around the cars, pretending to be interested in the equipment. . . ."

LA FRANCE AU TRAVAIL,
July 7, 1940

Elsewhere, it was the Germans who started conversations. M. Langeron's detailed eyewitness account of the period is extremely valuable:

"At 2 P.M. . . . . an open car with two German officers in it drew up in front of the left-hand terrace facing the Hôtel de Ville. . . . Their arrival drew a small crowd, and one of the officers addressed them in excellent French. He said: 'You are free, you can go where you like. We have no quarrel with you. The English dragged you into a war you'd lost before it even started. You'd like to have your husband back again, wouldn't you, madame?' 'Yes.' 'Well, my wife wants hers, too. Once we've signed the peace, we'll settle the English in a couple of weeks.'

"At 4:30 P.M., in the rue de Flandre, a German soldier, speaking very good French, declared: 'We have no quarrel with the French workers. They are our friends. Our battle is with the higher-ups.' As he spoke, he gestured significantly, and then added: 'The English are our enemies, but I haven't met one since the war started.' "[12]

Four days later, William L. Shirer, an American journalist passing through Paris, noted:

"I noticed today some open fraternizing between German troops and the inhabitants . . . Most of the German troops act like naïve tourists, and this has proved a pleasant surprise to the Parisians. It seems funny, but every German soldier carries a camera. I saw them by the thousands today, photographing Notre-Dame, the Arc de Triomphe, the Invalides. Thousands of German soldiers congregate all day long at the Tomb of the Unknown Soldier, where the flame still burns under the Arc. They bare their blond heads and stand there gazing."[13]

THE GERMANS INSTALL THEMSELVES

The German administration

The tall, blond, clear-eyed young men went away to die under other skies. In their place came potbellied gentlemen, whose severe military tunics betrayed unmistakably civilian contours. They were the economic and cultural occupation forces—scores and scores of them. They had long-winded titles, each as long and complicated as the next: Kriegsverwaltungschef, Oberkriegsverwaltungsrat, Sturmbannführer, not to mention the small fry, or Sonderführer, in their hundreds. They were installed in their positions according to a prearranged plan of long standing. Nothing had been left to chance. During the time that immediately followed the arrival of the Germans in Paris, there was some fluidity in the assigning of duties to the civilian and military authorities, and the distribution of their spheres of influence; but from the signing of the armistice onward, the complex workings of the occupation machine were finalized once and for all. I feel it is necessary, before beginning my account, to explain, if only in the most general terms, what these workings were.

The structure of the German military command can be compared to a pyramid. At its summit was the Militärbefehlshaber in Frankreich (Military High Command in France),[14] which controlled—in that they were delegated by the Commander-in-Chief of the Army, who, at that time, was General von Brauchitsch—all military, legislative and administrative powers throughout the country. Its main task was to insure the military security of the entire occupied territory, and to supervise and control all branches of the French economy and administration.

For this purpose, it had at its disposal two headquarters: military (Kommandostab) and administrative (Verwaltungsstab) installed in the Hôtel Majestic. The Kommandostab was put in command of Staff Colonel Speidel. One of its principal duties was to organize the control and supervision of the demarcation line between the two zones. It was equally responsible for the upkeep of roads, bridges, and so on. This was the work of three civilian organizations: Reichsarbeitsdienst, Technische Nothilfe, and—the most important of the three—Organisation Todt. It was further responsible for the supervision of prisoners, and for employing them, particularly in agricultural work. Finally, it had supreme control of the propaganda services, which under their group name of Propaganda Abteilung, were designed to condition French public opinion, and to keep the press, the movies and the theater "on the straight and narrow path." Three special departments were attached to the Kommandostab: they enjoyed a measure of autonomy, and Colonel Speidel merely coördinated their activities. These were: (1) The P.T.T. Services, which were the first to begin work again on the morning of the fourteenth, with the installation of a vast telegraphic network across Paris, and by taking over the Central Telephone Exchange in the rue des Archives; (2) the Billeting Services, under the control of Quartermaster General Jaennecke; (3) General Barkhausen's War Booty Services, which were responsible for drawing up a list of arms, equipment, ammunition, trucks, cars, and so on captured by the victors, and sending them to Germany.

The Verwaltungsstab was put under Dr. Schmid, Minister of the Interior and Economy in the Würtemberg government, and his deputy, the former President of the Wiesbaden Government, von Pfeffer, whose task it had been, since the invasion began, to repatriate millions of refugees, first in Holland, and later, in Belgium and France.

The Verwaltungsstab consisted of three divisions: (1) Internal Division: office administration and personnel. An essentially bureaucratic service, which had only slight connections outside. (2) Administrative Division. Its function was, according to the Germans themselves, "to safeguard the interests of the occupying powers, and not to promote schemes for internal order." Among its functions were included "collaboration" with the French police, control of municipal finance and of railways. In addition, it supervised teaching, libraries, records and museums. (3) Public Economy Division, which was the most important of the three. Its head was a senior civil servant from the German Ministry of State Economy, Dr. Michel, who was placed in charge of the French economy. The latter, according to the *Pariser Zeitung,* was to be given, for the first time, a planned organization ("planmässige Ausrichtung") based on the German model. Its main function was the "reshaping" of industrial and commercial enterprises, and their "aryanization." It controlled prices, dealt with the chemical industries, paper manufacture, and labor problems, as well as with credit, insurance, water, gas, coal and electric power; it covered everything.

To it was added a virtually autonomous service: the Office for the Supervision of French Banks, under the direction of the Bankpräsident, Dr. Carl Schaefer, who therefore took the title of High Commissioner to the Bank of France, where, in fact, he had his offices from June 29 onward.

Onto this already complicated machinery, with its

many ramifications, was grafted yet another part. The city of Paris, and the Paris region, comprising the departments of the Seine, Seine-et-Oise and Seine-et-Marne, were put under the military commander of Gross-Paris, General von Stutnitz, provisionally installed at the Hôtel Crillon, who was directly responsible to the Militärbefehlshaber previously referred to. He also had his administrative headquarters under Ministerialrat Rademacher, who had been recently praised for organizing the administration of Liège. The offices of the Verwaltungsstab, installed in the Palais-Bourbon, were put in charge of Staatsrat Turner. Oberkriegsverwaltungsrat Krüger, who was attached to the Hôtel de Ville, was in charge of the city of Paris' budget, and other special budgets connected with it: municipal taxes, public assistance, pawnshops, and so on. He also controlled the financial administration of the city's public utility companies (gas, water, electricity, the *métro*), markets covered by the city of Paris, and, generally speaking, all services depending directly or indirectly on the Paris municipality. Public assistance was delegated to a special section under Kriegsverwaltungsrat Prahlov; and Dr. Kreifeld, of similar rank, undertook liaison between the French municipal authorities and the German administration. That was not all. Subordinate to the commander of the Paris region was the commander of the city of Paris itself. This post, which was created by force of circumstances as soon as German troops entered Paris, was at first filled by General von Briesen, at the Hôtel Meurice. He was replaced after two weeks by a "specialist," General Schaumburg, who had been commander of Berlin from 1932 to 1936, and who was to combine the functions of commander of Greater Paris with that of the city itself.

Early regulations

As soon as he took office, General Stutnitz issued the following proclamation:

"People of Paris!

"German troops have occupied Paris.

"The city has been placed under military government.

"The military governor of the Paris region will take all measures necessary for the security of his forces and for the maintenance of order."

On June 20 (the sixth day of the occupation of Paris) there appeared an order from the Militärbefehlshaber that amounted to a kind of occupation charter—or rather, its penal code. Knowledge of this order will help the reader to follow more easily later turns of events:

"The German army guarantees the inhabitants absolute personal safety and safeguard of their possessions. Those who act calmly and peacefully have nothing to fear.

"All acts of violence and sabotage will be punished with

the utmost severity. Acts of sabotage are held to include any damage to—or misappropriation of—crops, military provisions and installations of any kind, as well as the defacing of posters belonging to the occupying powers. Gas, water, and power installations, railways, canal locks and art treasures are under the personal supervision of the occupying army.

"Any persons found guilty of the following acts will be answerable to the War Tribunal:

"1. Any aid given to non-German combatants in occupied territories.

"2. Any aid given to civilians attempting to escape to non-occupied territories.

"3. Any giving of information to the detriment of the German army or the Reich, to persons or authorities outside the occupied territories.

"4. Any contact with prisoners.

"5. Any offense against the German army and its leaders.

"6. Street gatherings, the distribution of leaflets, public meetings and demonstrations not previously approved by the German High Command.

"7. Any incitement to absenteeism, deliberate refusal to work, strikes or lockouts.

"The public services, police and schools will function normally. . . . Directors and heads will be responsible to the occupying powers for the reliability of their services.

"All enterprises, businesses and banks will continue to operate. . . . Any unjustified closing down will be punished.

"Any hoarding of articles in daily use is forbidden, and will be considered as an act of sabotage. . . .

"Any raising of prices and salaries above the level existing on the first day of the occupation is prohibited.

"The rate of exchange is fixed as follows: one French franc equals 0.05 Reichsmarks. . . . German money will be accepted.

"The German armed forces will pay for their purchases

in cash. For sums over 500 Reichsmarks (10,000 francs), delivery notes will be given. Accounts will be settled by the German Military Administration."

At the end of the following month, this order was supplemented by several more emphasizing certain details.

The one of July 15 deserves special mention:

"1. Art treasures will not be removed from their present places, or modified in any way, without written permission from the Militärverwaltung.

"2. Transfers of art treasures, to be valid, must be authorized by myself.

"3. Art treasures, whose value exceeds 100,000 francs, must be reported in writing by their owners or custodians by August 15, 1940."

The real implications of this measure will shortly become clear.

THE RETURN TO PARIS

Every Frenchman responsible

From the moment the occupation began, the Germans ran into innumerable problems, one of which turned out to be particularly complex. During the exodus, families had been broken up. People were wandering about the roads in utter confusion, tramping from one place to another, parents separated from their children, husbands from their wives. In Paris, President von Pfeffer's offices were inundated with requests and complaints. As the offices were hard to enter, petitioners, especially women, used the newspapers to air their grievances. The German authorities reacted unfavorably, and sent the press a kind of official communiqué whose contents are worth careful attention:

"The French papers are becoming increasingly concerned with the refugee problem, implying that its solution is solely a matter for the occupation forces.

"We Germans are aware of the misery and suffering of these refugees, and we are familiar with the appalling consequences of their plight. But the fact that, being a civilized nation, we have done what we could to alleviate this misery and distress, should not encourage the French to blame Germany for the terrible hardships these refugees have suffered.

"We feel obliged to remind all Frenchmen that they must not forget that it was France that declared war on Germany—France which used to boast of being a country run on liberal principles, France which was, so to speak, the very incarnation of democracy.

"We are in no sense wrong to conclude that this insane declaration of war is the responsibility not only of the country's leaders, but of every individual Frenchman who voted them into power.

"In fact, in accordance with the rules of the game of democracy—as every Frenchman liked to put it—it would have been simple for the people to place other men at their country's head; and the French people will understand that it is not in our power to absolve them of their undoubted responsibility for the sad plight of the refugees . . .

"The French people, therefore, have no reason to attack Germany. They will do better to protest to those who alone are the guilty ones—that is, the members of the French government."

LE MATIN,
July 30, 1940

This "clarification" left no room for ambiguity. The French were unequivocally told that they were held personally responsible for having plunged their country into an "insane war," which implied that they had to be ready to take the consequences; and that if they had been spared the punishment they deserved, they owed it to the mercy and magnanimity of their conquerors.

Meanwhile, the main preoccupation of the German authorities was that the people who had left Paris should return as quickly as possible. Since the German entry, there were about 700,000 inhabitants, as compared with the 2,879,746 registered at the 1936 census. It was therefore necessary to recover more than two million people.

The German services were actively engaged in transporting some by truck, and supplying others, who had cars, with gasoline coupons, renewable at successive stages of the journey. The Vichy government was called upon to arrange special trains for those who were returning to the occupied zone. The result was that by the end of three weeks, about 300,000 Parisians had made their way back, and the census that was taken in Paris on July 7, the twenty-fourth day of the occupation, credited the capital with 1,051,306 inhabitants, of whom only 160,000 belonged to "middle-class" districts (first, second, sixth, seventh, eighth, ninth and sixteenth *arrondissements*).

The result was that, while the working-class districts were more or less back to normal, that part of the capital lying between the Opéra and the porte Maillot—especially from the place de la Concorde onward—had the appearance of a huge, desolate wasteland.

Paris comes back to life

A woman from Neuilly, who took a walk in the Champs-Élysées on June 15, noted:

"All one sees in this deserted city, which looks so sad with its closed stores, are green and gray-blue uniforms."

The following day, the sixteenth, "there were more people about," according to M. Langeron, "especially in the afternoon."[15]

A woman from the fourteenth *arrondissement* also went out, and decided to visit the Champs-Élysées:

"Went back to the Colisée and took a corner table. Several Germans were sitting there. Some of the women were already smiling in their direction. A few days ago, they were smiling at French officers and French soldiers. It was an unpleasant sight, and I preferred not to look.

"On the way home, I passed the Invalides. When I saw German sentries there, I began to cry. My country is really done for."

LA RÉVOLUTION NATIONALE,
November 9, 1941

A journalist on *Le Matin,* after walking around the boulevards on the following day, the seventeenth, felt most optimistic:

"A number of cafés have raised their iron shutters and have set out their terraces again. . . . When you consider that several movie houses have already reopened, and that public services, such as gas, water and electricity, have kept going, as has the *métro,* Paris life is obviously well on the way back to normal. . . . As for the big stores, they haven't been closed for a single day. . . . The window displays may not have been perfect, there may have been some confusion in odd departments, there may have been fewer assistants, but the customers didn't seem to notice.

"In the cosmetics, furnishing and clothing departments, women were buying things, fingering materials, chatting away . . ."

LE MATIN,
June 18, 1940

On the same day, M. Langeron remembered:

"The streets seemed more lively yesterday, with new stores opening up. There were a good many customers on the café terraces."[16]

On Sunday, June 23 (the second Sunday of the occupation), he noted:

"There has been a great increase in the number of people walking in the main streets, in public gardens, and sitting on café terraces."[17]

The same day, William L. Shirer, already quoted, decided to take "a little, 'Sentimental Journey' " across Paris with a friend. These were his impressions (in the book previously cited):

"(We set off on) foot, because there are no cars, busses, or taxis. We walked down through the Place Vendôme and thought of Napoleon. Pushed on through the Tuileries. It made my heart feel a little better to see so many children about. They were playing on the seesaws. The merry-go-round was turning with its load of children . . .

"It was an exquisite June day . . .

"Then (we walked on) through the Louvre and across the Seine. The fishermen were dangling their lines from the bank, as always. I thought: 'Surely this will go on to the end of Paris, to the end of time . . .'

"Then (we walked on) down the Seine to Notre-Dame. The sandbags had been removed from the central portal . . . Inside the Cathedral the light was too strong, with the original rose window and the two transept windows out. But from up the river as we had approached, the view of the façade, the Gothic in all its glory, was superb . . .

"Then (we walked on to) the Panthéon, from the boulevard Saint-Michel, and then through the Luxembourg Gardens, as lovely as ever, and crowded with children, as ever, which cheered me up again . . .

"And then Montparnasse, with apértifs on the sidewalk of the Rotonde, and then the Dôme across the street as jammed with crackpots as ever, and in front of us a large table full of middle-aged French women of the bourgoisie, apparently recovering from the daze, because their anger was rising at the way the little *gamins* (*elles sont françaises, aprés tout!*) were picking up the German soldiers . . . And then to our hotel, filled with German soldiers . . ."

The author, who made himself out to be an inveterate Parisian, obviously did not seem to know what sort of "young girls" walked along the boulevard du Montparnasse at apéritif time. . . .

Three days later, the director of *L'Illustration,* who had withdrawn to Bordeaux, returned to Paris to investigate the chances of again publishing his magazine there. Back in Bordeaux, he described his impressions to his readers:

"At about eleven in the morning, Paris livened up a bit, but there still weren't many people about. . . . We passed companies of unarmed Germans marching down the main boulevards, singing in time to their steps. Flags with swastikas on them were flying from every monument. . . . Twelve thousand French policemen had remained to keep order, which was perfect . . . They were controlling the traffic with stiff, mechanical hand-signals."

July 7, 1940

This was a new, German-style discipline for hand-signals, which the occupation authorities had insisted on from the first day.

One of his colleagues who accompanied him also recorded his impressions:

"In the smart restaurants, menus were still large and varied. But they were used almost exclusively by German officers. In the one where I lunched, for about fifty francs, I was the only Frenchman. . . .

"Toward the end of the afternoon, I went to Maxim's,

to the Colisée and Fouquet's. Those typically Parisian cafés were meeting places for the senior ranks of the German garrison—majors, colonels and generals. Truth compels me to admit that there was, as usual, no shortage of women. That didn't surprise me. On the other hand, I was somewhat amazed to see a busload of German tourists, both men and women, in the Champs-Élysées. 'Trips to Paris' had already begun. German travel agencies weren't wasting any time!"

L'ILLUSTRATION,
July 13, 1940

This avalanche of "tourists" was also mentioned, on July 2, by Jean Texcier, who later wrote the famous *Conseils à un occupé:*

"I was dropped off that morning in the Gare d'Austerlitz—what irony!—in a vast desert teeming with jackboots. Everywhere were huge flags with swastikas on them, and I could see the enemy cheerfully smiling at what he imagined was Paris, dashing off in busloads, armed with cameras, to historic monuments. Parisians, still a bit nervous, but already acclimatized, stared curiously at the sprinkling of gray and green uniforms; and young women, eager for new sensations, ventured conversations in cafés. A dreadful press had already been set up in the city."[18]

We will now discuss this "dreadful press."

BIRTH OF THE "OCCUPIED" PRESS

Appearance of the Presse-Gruppe

It has been mentioned previously that one of Colonel Speidel's Kommandostab divisions was devoted to propaganda—or rather, to the "conditioning" of French public opinion through the press, radio, theater, movies, and so on. According to Dr. Goebbels' *Journal,* this was a dirty trick played on him by von Ribbentrop, the Foreign Minister. Ribbentrop's aim was to keep this important sphere out of his colleague's clutches, because he found Goebbels "over-Germanic" and too liable to offend French sensibilities. In any case, this branch remained under the wing of the Hôtel Majestic until the occupation ended, and although it was regularly inspired by Dr. Goebbels, the vacillations and misconstructions that resulted made him regret the absence of a single, all-powerful propaganda chief in Paris.

The Presse-Gruppe (Press Group) of the Propaganda-Staffel[19] began to operate on about the twenty-fifth of June.[20] But *Le Matin,* which had suspended publication on the eleventh, had already reappeared on the seventeenth, followed five days later by an imitation of *Paris-Soir.* Immediately after German troops had entered Paris, a press attaché from the Tenth Army, Lieutenant Weber, who before the war had been director of the Deutsches Nachrichten Bureau (a German news agency, usually known by the initials "D.N.B."), contacted the proprietor of *Le Matin,* Maurice Bunau-Varilla, who had remained in Paris. The old man was extremely coöperative, and apparently saw to it personally that his printing machines were put to work again.[21]

"Monsieur Bunau-Varilla," Lieutenant Weber said to him, "I expect your paper, under your personal supervision, to serve the truth objectively."[22] The German truth, presumably.

The second stage involved the setting up of an evening paper. The story has often been told of how Lieutenant Weber was given the keys of the *Paris-Soir* building by an old elevator operator, Schieslé, an Alsatian, who had been left there with two others, (a Swiss and a Swede) after the staff of the paper had been evacuated. His former chief, Pierre Lazareff, introduced him in his book, previously quoted, as a kind of "Gestapo private-eye," planted in *Paris-Soir* long before the war to spy on what the staff was saying and doing. Jean Quéval, author of a very well organized, fully documented book on the "occupied" press, saw him more as a poor wretch who, promoted to director-general of a large daily newspaper, revealed an astonishing capacity for administration.[23] The reader can decide for himself. Schieslé held office for nearly three months. Jean Quéval also told the following story:

"Before returning to obscurity, Schieslé met, one September day, a close friend of Jean Prouvost's. 'Sir,' he told him, 'I am M. Prouvost's loyal and devoted servant. I used to earn 3,500 francs a month. For two months now, as director-general, I have been getting 5,000. The extra money is not mine by right.' Upon which he took out a wallet and counted out the additional salary he had earned from his directorial activities."

It should be mentioned that *La Victoire* reappeared on the same day as *Le Matin.* It was owned by Gustave Hervé, and had been a shambles long before the war. He used his remaining stocks of paper to print an edition on June 17, in which he advised moderation toward Hitler and pleaded with Parisians not to treat the Germans as "Huns." After three days, he was told his paper would not be required. Similarly, little notice need be taken of the *Dernières Nouvelles de Paris,* which first appeared on June 20 in the shape of a financial agency paper, and which sank into oblivion on the following September 16.

The third stage is represented by *La France au travail,* which first appeared on June 30.[24] By this time the Presse-Gruppe was operating, and was, in fact, behind the launching of this enterprise. It was introduced by the slogan, "Salvation Through Work."

"The present crisis gives us a chance to reorganize completely. Better to change today what cannot be changed tomorrow."

This succinct declaration was followed by a declaration of faith that did not fail to puzzle many readers:

"A group of French workers demands:

"1. The freeing of all their comrades imprisoned for defending the peace.

"2. The accusation and public trial of all those who plunged France into war.

"3. The confiscation of all war benefits, the institution of a huge levy on big fortunes, and national control of banks, mines, large firms and railways.

"4. The reactivation of all businesses, even those whose owners have gone away."

"It's *L'Humanité* again, in disguise," people thought. The deception worked at first, but it lasted only a few days.

After launching three dailies, the Presse-Gruppe undertook the launching of a literary weekly. This was *La Gerbe.* The first number came out on July 11. It was introduced in these terms:

"We shall not indulge in polemics; we intend to look inward, because we all carry on our shoulders a burden of responsibility for the disaster. . . .

"We shall neither accuse nor vilify, nor support one party more than another. Past faults, whether conscious or not, will not be dwelt on. What we want is that those who have committed crimes shall remain silent, both they and their kind. That we demand. But no word of hatred shall pass our lips; hatred is negative, not creative, and what we want are positive forces.

"Let us go forward! Let men of good will in all parties join us! We have but one rallying cry: 'France . . .' Modern conditions call out for modern men and modern methods."

This, too, was a concoction by the Presse-Gruppe experts. It was less obvious than the previous one, but managed at first to create some confusion. The following appeared in the issue of the eighteenth of July:

"In the last few days, a number of newsboys, calling out the name of *La Gerbe,* have been adding something of their own to edify the passers-by: *'La Gerbe, ex-Gringoire!'* while others have shouted the name: *'La Gerbe, ex-Humanité!'*

"We are neither *La Gringoire* nor *L'Humanité. . . .* We are the humble and obedient servants of the only law of life that exists. Only those who have never lived intensely will find this expression vague. A wise and ancient adage has it: 'It is not for man to decide where he is going.' That, gentlemen, is our function!"

Finally, to complete our picture: In order to fit in with Dr. Goebbels' imperative needs, there had to be a violently anti-Semitic fighting organ, in the style of Julius Streicher's *Stürmer.* (Streicher was the most savage "Judenfresser" [Jew-eater] of the Third Reich.) This was *Au Pilori,* which will be referred to later.

Private enterprises

The Presse-Gruppe's activities seemed to end there. But there were private enterprises, as for instance, *Aujourd'hui,* which had originally been financed by a rich patron, and whose actual production was entrusted to two professional journalists who managed, through personal contacts, to form a team of talented writers much to the public taste. The Presse-Gruppe was very sympathetic and readily gave permission for its formation. It predicted that this new publication would become a malleable instrument like the rest, and that the founders could be discharged as soon as they had finished the job of setting it on its feet.

Requests for authorization were not always so easily granted; in fact, they were sometimes not granted at all, in spite of the applicant's protestations of "respectability" and "racial purity."

This is what the director of the big fashion magazine, *Vogue,* had to say on the subject. *Vogue* was

American-owned, but its Paris edition was run by various French corporations. He wanted permission to reappear in mid-July. He wrote:

"I went to the headquarters of the Propaganda-Staffel to try my luck. I was given an appointment for an interview with the Sonderführer, or Vice-Chief of the propaganda division in charge of the illustrated press.

"A surprise awaited me. I found myself face to face with a fellow who had, for years before the war, been a free-lance photographer in the fashion field around Paris. Since at *Vogue* we had a regular staff of really top-flight photographers, and I had thought this man's work of no special distinction, we had never purchased any pictures from him. He had left Paris at the beginning of the war in September, 1939. Now it turned out he was Lieutenant Maier of the German Army Reserve . . .

"Lieutenant Maier rather enjoyed the surprise he gave me. His mustache perked up and his eyes glistened behind his thick spectacles as I discussed the resumption of publication. I was anxious to get permission quickly, for various favored intermediaries of the Germans were seizing titles and launching publications under the appropriated names.

"I was given a formidable list of conditions I must meet, including the presentation of documentary proof that our publication had 'no Jewish capital or attachments.' I was also obliged to give a full list of biographical information on all those I intended to re-employ. For weeks I shuttled faithfully between my offices and the Staffel headquarters, doing what was asked of me, but getting no response . . .

"At this period I was several times approached by intermediaries who thought they might be able to 'arrange things.' A call I had from the French owner of a bindery, a man I had known previously in business, was typical. He protested profusely that he was terribly embarrassed, that he would not have come on this errand except that he wanted to do me a service. He knew someone who could, he thought, get me permission to publish.

" 'I'm no worse off than the others,' I told him.

" 'Well, others have obtained permission. I don't think you've seen the right people.'

" 'I've seen everybody I've been told to see.'

" 'Yes, but if you would cooperate I think it could be arranged.'

"When it became clear that the crux of the matter was financial, I said pointedly that perhaps too much cooperation might be required. The bindery owner went off with a saddened air and said he'd 'let me know.' I never saw him again. But while our organization remained paralyzed in the German bureaucratic web, a minor fashion paper, *Art et la Mode,* which had a prewar circulation of about 3,500 against our French sale of 40,000, appeared in lavish new dress. It was as nearly *Vogue* as it could be within the limits of the taste of its editor . . . (who) frankly confided to the couturiers that she 'had the mission of replacing *Vogue.*' "[25]

But there were some who returned to the fold. *L'Illustration* came back to Paris in the first two weeks of August. *L'Oeuvre* followed about mid-September, and *Le Petit Parisien* at the beginning of November. Meanwhile, Doriot had assembled a number of Communist party renegades and launched his *Cri du peuple;* and Jean Luchaire, too, had managed to persuade the Germans that Paris needed a large evening paper of high intellectual standing. This was *Les Nouveaux Temps.*

Publicity schemes

It would be an exaggeration to say that all these publications, even though they were serving the same cause, were bound by close family ties. No opportunity to run down a colleague was neglected. What mattered most was attracting a public, luring it with all sorts of publicity schemes. *La France au travail* decided to appeal for its readers' active coöperation. Little good came of this, to judge from the editorial comment that appeared on the third of August:

"The Editors have received countless offers, both verbal and written, of coöperation on a wide range of subjects. They regret that owing to practical considerations, they are unable to reply to all the letters . . .

"We have also had to discontinue visits, except in special circumstances."

Aujourd'hui found something different. This "typically Parisian" paper made up questions that a woman journalist put to strangers she accosted while walking around the streets. Their photographs would then appear in the paper.

Here are examples:

"In the event of prices being illegally raised, should shops be closed, or should the guilty boss be replaced by a manager?

"Are you for or against doing away with the Légion d'Honneur?

"Do you agree that *métro* tickets should not be required by the few French soldiers still in Paris?

"Should overdue taxes be paid?

"Should people do physical exercises in the mornings?

"Men with beards—do you sleep with them over or under the sheet?

"Are you for or against make-up?

"Do you believe in Santa Claus, and what do you want him to bring you?

"Is the bowler hat on its way out?

"To make it easier to get to Montparnasse, which would you prefer: an automatic elevator, an escalator, or a mountain railway?

"What is your opinion of workers being given a small glass of alcohol every morning?"

Apparently, the question about bearded men's sleeping habits was the most successful, and created great interest among Parisians.

Paris-Soir went about things more intelligently and showed it was both astute and observant. It exploited the ordeals and miseries that the people of Paris were undergoing. This came under the heading "mutual aid." In its first number, it appealed to readers:

"Families must not lose hope. Use and exploit the columns of *Paris-Soir,* which will publish regularly and tirelessly all appeals received."

The terrible agony from which nearly all these families suffered was in not knowing what had happened to prisoners-of-war. On July 17, *Paris-Soir* undertook to forward to them any parcels it received. In August, it was the unemployment problem that supplied a pretext for a new publicity campaign. After the census of January 4, 1941, there were, in fact, 171,738 unemployed in Paris, and 164,424 in the suburbs—in all, 336,162 were without work (see the *Pariser Zeitung,* January 21, 1941). A free "Situations Wanted" column was offered, and at the same time a series of social functions was initiated with the object of helping the needy.

This began on September 15, with a nautical competition on the Seine for the benefit of a prisoner-of-war fund. Then there was a charity gala at the A.B.C. for children, victims of the exodus; another at the Théâtre Pigalle for prisoners; others at the Opèra, the Gaumont-Palace, in fashionable nightspots and restaurants, and so on. Medical aid, wartime adoptions, and social clubs were organized. The staff of *Paris-Soir* went to work on several fronts.[26]

Results soon came in. In November, 1940, *Paris-Soir* ran to 970,000 copies, while *Le Petit Parisien* made only 689,000 and *Le Matin* 532,000; *Aujourd'hui* hardly passed 110,000 and *La France au travail,* 92,000. As for Jean Luchaire's "large evening paper of high intellectual standing," it barely scraped 30,000.[27]

The point was that *Paris-Soir,* like *Le Matin* and *Le Petit Parisien,* sold well, but people had grown wary. Granted they had always said, "You don't want to believe everything you read in the papers," and, "All journalists are liars"; at that time, the reaction of the man-in-the-street was, "It's all a lot of propaganda."

On July 1, *La France au travail* wrote:

"The other day, in Montparnasse, some people were standing around a car listening to the radio. I heard one of them observe: 'They can say what they like. It's all propaganda!'

"The day after, I heard the same words from a passer-by who had just bought a paper: 'It's all a lot of propaganda!'

"At one time, Parisians were credulous to a fault; now they have become suspicious. . . . They imagine everyone wants to exploit and impress them."

Propaganda and pâtisseries

Dr. Hermann Eich, head of the Presse-Gruppe, reports he was astonished at first by the ignorance of Paris journalists concerning international politics, and he stated that it was for this reason that German propaganda services began to organize press conferences. He even claimed that, in the early days, several journalists used to come to the Presse-Gruppe offices to ask what and how they should write. This may be true, because there were some who were afraid to displease their new bosses, and thought it wiser to ask them beforehand how they wanted to be served.

These conferences were held twice a week, on Tuesday and Friday mornings on the premises of the

Propaganda-Staffel. Overcramped at the Majestic, it had moved into the handsome National City Bank building, 52, avenue des Champs-Élysées, allotted to them by the German commander. The "president," a Sonderführer from the Presse-Gruppe, (heads of services only spoke on very important occasions) summarized what the German newspapers—particularly the *Völkischer Beobachter*—had said the day before, indicating what topics should be mentioned. He did not actually dictate the article word for word, but was sure to hand around, whenever necessary, a "kindly insert" item, which had to be reproduced accurately and uncut. There were also movie shows to which journalists were invited. These took place in the basement of the Propaganda-Staffel building, in the presence of a Sonderführer, who was seated in a raised armchair at one end of the room, as if on a balcony. German newsreels were shown, as well as "cultural films" shot in Berlin. Spectators had to sign a register placed at the entrance. M. Dubois, a journalist, recalled in his book, quoted previously:

"When the main film was too boring, some of them would try to slip out for a breath of air in the Champs-Élysées. What a hope! These weaklings had to give up the idea, because the doors were secured with heavy chains and padlocks. When we showed our amazement at being locked in, we had to be satisfied with the following answer: 'It is feared that terrorists may attempt to throw bombs into the room during the performance. We are doing this for your protection.' "[28]

Bimonthly tea parties in the Press Club started by the Propaganda-Staffel were more popular. Here is Edmond Dubois again:

"A headwaiter, obviously a policeman, received visitors with an obsequious smile. The place consisted of three or four large rooms and the walls were covered with slogans from the fertile mind of Dr. Goebbels, asserting that the future of the world depended on the efforts of the press. . . . Journalists were grouped at small tables, drinking cups of real coffee; waiters, behaving in a manner suitable to the serving of such a rare beverage and such welcome food, handed around plates of cakes, each guest being allotted a *mille-feuille,* a cream-puff and a pastry. Sugar was unlimited. But the Propaganda-Staffel would have thought the refreshments wasted if they had no propaganda value. The 'coffee tea-party' was the excuse for some artistic performance. Each corner of Europe supplied a troupe of singers or dancers. . . . There was a Danish reunion, a Belgian reunion, a Hungarian reunion, and a recital by a Parisian singer. She was a magnificent woman, talented and dynamic, and the mistress of some higher-up in the Propaganda-Staffel (at least that's what they were whispering at the table where I was sitting)."[29]

In this way, a team of experts in psychological warfare managed, in a few months, to forge a multi-edged weapon with which it intended to tame—or, to use its own expression, "regenerate"—public spirit in Paris.

LIFE RETURNS TO NORMAL

Those who stayed and those who went

People began to come back: civil servants, writers, journalists, actors, magistrates, professors, society women and demimondaines.

Streetwalkers, and prostitutes in brothels, had mostly remained in Paris. On the morning of June 14, the day German troops entered Paris, a notice could be seen on the door of the well-known establishment in the rue Chabanais: "Business as usual from 3 P.M."[30]

As for civil servants, *La France au travail* wrote:

"The first civil servants to go back to work in the capital were from the Treasury. . . . Wouldn't it have been more logical to have the P.T.T. workers, or better still, the post office and bank workers, back first?"

July 5, 1940

Both men and women were faced with a formidable problem: that of adapting themselves to new conditions. For some it was a question of exploiting the situation as best they could; for others, a question of easing their difficulties. Those who returned to the fold were somewhat ungraciously welcomed by the press. In the returning flood of Parisians, it detected some possible competition.

"The Scum Returns"; this was the title of an article with which *Au Pilori* welcomed them home. It read:

"The dregs of Paris are back among us again; look around the streets, cafés and restaurants, look at their revolting little prewar faces, puffy with big business lunches, their shifty eyes, and their dirty little fingers that have been poking around God knows where. I know some newspapers in Paris where these scum have been hanging around, back to their old tricks again, 'regrouping' and cooking up their little schemes and plans of attack."

September 13, 1940

About this time there began a clash of interests, and a confrontation between two different points of view:

some believed, or pretended they believed, that a new age was beginning for France; others sought merely to repair the damage and to revert to their old, comfortable ways of life. Those who had stayed in Paris regarded those who had left as pathetic cowards; those who had left regarded those who stayed as "fifth columnists" revealed in their true colors. An article in *La France au travail* clearly reflected this attitude:

"To hear some of the people who've come back, you'd think nothing had happened.

"I run across them every day, looking fresh and relaxed, and the first thing they say is:

" 'Well, what have you been doing since the evacuation?'

"When I answer, 'I just stayed in Paris,' they look at me as if I were part of the 'fifth column' . . .

"The ones who panicked, and took to their heels and fled to save their precious skins and possessions, treat those who stayed as highly suspect.

"It's a wonder they don't actually mention the word treason."

LA FRANCE AU TRAVAIL,
September 18, 1940

The same paper warned its readers against those who returned:

"Fellow Parisians, open your eyes—open them wide, as they say.

"If you stayed at home in the hour of crisis, when there was some merit and courage in doing so, don't let yourselves be taken in by the returning mob, with their outstretched hands and smiling faces. . . . Those who dashed off to Vichy and elsewhere have no right to a place in Paris.

"We won't allow it.

"We've had just about enough of their little tricks."

Those who came back and found their apartments and belongings safe and sound were clearly delighted. This infuriated *Au Pilori:*

"The well-to-do, lily-livered middle classes of last June, and what's left of the upper classes, are already back to normal. Yes, my friends, they're playing bridge again; they're holding receptions in my lady's drawing room, and —you can see for yourselves—they're riding in the Bois de Boulogne again. . . . And they're stuffing themselves with their cakes, their little fingers crooked. Once again, they're failing to understand, to feel; once again they're leading useless, cowardly lives, as dead as mutton. . . ."

September 13, 1940

A contributor to *Aujourd'hui,* in an attempt to explain the capital's new climate, invented this conversation between two Parisians:

"So you're satisfied, eh?"

"Yes, I'm quite satisfied."

"Of course. You're not hard to please."

"It's hardly the moment to be."

"You watch out! It's a crime to be wise and do nothing."

"Must you preach? As if we hadn't had enough! Be reasonable."

"How can you be, when you see what Paris is like this autumn, after we've only just been defeated? Anyone with his heart in the right place ought to feel sick at the sight of all these cafés, movie houses and music halls."

"Things are getting back to normal."

"Exactly. People are eating and drinking, enjoying themselves, getting back to their dirty little games again; you wouldn't think France had been torn to pieces. You can see their foxy faces sniffing away: all the little predatory beasts on the scent again. Not forgetting the big ones, either, hiding away in their burrows now that they've defiled our national heritage. There are even some who've stuffed themselves, and are already digesting."

"Not so fast."

September 23, 1940

Shows for all tastes

The Germans wanted Paris to reassume, as quickly as possible, its character of the "City of Light." The Propaganda-Staffel theater group made active preparations. Movie houses led the way. Three large movie houses in the Champs-Élysées (the Triomphe, the Colisée, and the Portiques), as well as two small newsreel theatres, had been open to the public since the twenty-third of June. The Marignan was reserved for German troops. On July 19, *Le Matin* wrote:

"Nearly all the movie houses on the boulevards are open. For ten francs or even less, you can sit in the best seats of a large first-run movie house. It's true there aren't any more first-run films, and the ones shown are at least a few months —if not a few years—old. But the public is satisfied."

The music halls were the first to open, with programs thrown together indiscriminately. That did not matter. The important thing was to have some big, dramatic productions. Jouvet had just returned. He made a sensational statement:

"The time has come for a reorganization and remolding of our work in the theater. Until now we have shrunk from hacking away at some of the tough old crusts that have accrued with the years. Now these protective shells are cracked wide open."

Aujourd'hui, quoting his words, declared:

"One of our dramatic hearths is blazing again."

September 11, 1940

This "hearth" first blazed at the Théâtre des Ambassadeurs. It was, according to the press of the day, "a great Parisian event."

The theater critic of *La Gerbe* was moved to write as follows:

"Abroad, we have an unchallenged reputation for frivolity. Today, in Paris, in the entertainment world, we seem to be doing all we can to impress on German officers and men now in the capital an image of Paris and ourselves that sustains this legend. This legend does not, however, have anything to do with the real France.

"We talk ourselves into accepting the fact that the nude—the lovely, alluring nude—is everywhere so popular just now, or that certain strip-tease shows are idiotic and appallingly shoddy, though we are slightly ashamed of it. The Germans, we tell ourselves, know these shows have been hastily flung together; they'll make allowances. They will realize these exhibitions have been put on for them, because, alas, to many people, Paris is famous for the beauty of a few shapely hips. But in the theatrical world, the situation is more serious. The Comédie Française and the Odéon are closed, and won't be open for a month. What, then, is left?

"All that is left is what some people have called 'the theatrical event,' symbolizing 'the rebirth of Paris.' I refer to M. Michel Duran's *Nous ne sommes pas mariés,* which opened with a splash at the Ambassadeurs.

"Since there are no others, this is the play on the basis of which the Germans will judge how good the Paris theater is. You can see for yourselves: for three acts, you sit there, while a man decides whether or not he'll deceive his mistress. In this age of tragedy, the spectator is confronted with the agonizing dilemma of whether it's better if you deceive your wife discreetly, or make her unhappy letting her know you desire another woman. . . . After which, we shall probably take offense, and scream at the tops of our lungs because we're considered frivolous. . . ."

LA GERBE,
August 1, 1940

At the Bouffes-Parisiens, *Phi-Phi* was revived. Wasn't it inevitable? . . . *La France au travail* thought otherwise:

"We would be very wrong, you see, to despair. We didn't feel that the French were equal to the disaster they had so conscientiously been expecting. We thought they lacked courage and imagination, could never recover and fight back. Not a bit of it! France mustn't be judged by her panic of last June. The sun isn't judged during an eclipse. Forget those unhappy memories. Today, thank God, we are shaking off our apathy. We are almost ourselves again. We shall soon be restored again to the world's favor!

"*Phi-Phi* has reopened. . . .

"Before returning to the monarchy, we return to the operetta. We exhibit female nudes—never enough of them! We may have lost Metz and other towns, but we still have Willemetz, and that's comfort enough. . . ."

September 25, 1940

The German propaganda services thought they had detected a passion among Parisians for military music, and organized an increasing number of concerts and recitals all over the place: in the place de l'Opéra, in the Tuileries Gardens, in front of Notre Dame, in the place de la République, and so on. There were always enough idlers willing to listen to military marches, two thousand or more waiting in the place de la République on July 24, according to M. Langeron, a hodgepodge of utterly unknown—and deservedly so—German composers, with snippets of Wagner and Beethoven incongruously tacked on. One young girl complained to her cousin on the staff of *Aujourd'hui* that "some fool" had "squeezed her waist" while she was listening to the funeral march from the *Götterdammerung* (September 14, 1940).

Special mention must be made of cabarets and night clubs. With the blessing of the High Command, Paris immediately became a furlough center to which soldiers could go and relax. Though other ranks had to be content with bus tours, movie shows, and being entertained in "establishments" strictly controlled by the Occupation Forces Health Services, officers had the complete run of Paris night life. And—need it be said—they made as good use of it as their very liberal supplies of marks permitted.

A special map of Paris, divided into three areas (Montmartre, Montparnasse and the Champs-Élysées), showed where the officially "recommended" night clubs were located. The *Pariser Zeitung,* a newspaper for Germans in Paris, printed it conspicuously twice: on the fifth and the thirteenth of April, 1941. Naturally, the owners of these establishments were on extremely good terms with the occupation authorities, and were given a number of welcome concessions, especially in matters of food supplies, and, what was otherwise highly complicated, heating.

Reporting a delivery of eight tons of coal a month to the Boeuf sur le toit, *Le Franciste,* on December 13, 1941, commented ironically: "Clients will keep nice and warm."

The clients, of course, were mainly from the German army, but they included a number of Parisians, such as black marketeers or agents for the Wehrmacht supply services.

There were different sorts of cabarets. Some merely provided a floor show; at others, you could eat and drink. Some shut at curfew time; others stayed open all night. As Edmond Dubois wrote:

"In night clubs which proudly boasted 'Floor Show From 9 P.M. Till Dawn,' they had a special technique for delaying the customers. This consisted of taking hours to ice the champagne, or delaying bringing the check to people who wanted to leave early. Ten minutes in a club near the place Blanche meant a sleepless night. From midnight till five o'clock, a night club became a kind of commercial police station."[31]

The industry became highly developed. *L'Illustration,* applauding the fact, wrote:

"Never before has Paris had so many cabarets. It is a good thing that the tradition is being carried on. There is enough sorrow and unhappiness in the world for some, without others being deprived of their pleasures and gaieties."

January 10, 1942

A contributor to *Aujourd'hui,* welcoming Marshal Pétain's wife to Paris, addressed her in these words:

"Isn't Paris smart and well turned out? You may have heard complaints about excesses in some of her fashionable night clubs. I feel sure you were not shocked. Necessities must be catered to. Paris owes her glory to spiritual values, but also to the brilliance of some of her amusements. It's just a question of keeping up sophisticated appearances, which the experts assure us are mercifully superficial."

March 30, 1941

We will now attempt a Grand Tour of the new "Paris bei Nacht," through articles and gossip columns from "occupied" newspapers:

In the Champs-Élysées, Sa Majesté, adjoining a famous restaurant, had a distinguished clientele.

"The décor is in warm, red tones. You eat to the music of an excellent orchestra, but the evening can go on very late. It is accompanied by a constant flow of first-class attractions."

L'ILLUSTRATION,
January 3–10, 1942

Next, the Lido. *La Gerbe* stated emphatically:

"Personally, we can think of nowhere in Paris more pleasant than the Lido for what is oddly named a 'dinner show.' The food is good, the girls lovely, and both are stylishly presented."

July 2, 1943

Aujourd'hui praised the languorous charms of the L'Aiglon, which was one of the first to reopen:

A German soldier buys a copy of "La Victoire."

Café de la Paix, June 1940.

Return of the ashes of l'Aiglon, December 15, 1940.

French postcard satirically commenting
on the use of occupation troops.

"L'Aiglon is in the Champs-Élysées—where else?—a stronghold of Parisian atmosphere. A place where you can forget the vexing questions of the present day—unless, of course, you go there to revive prewar memories and friendships. Discreet pleasure can be enjoyed in the company of the Duke of Reichstadt's portrait."

September 13, 1940

Near the Étoile, the Night Club, according to *La Gerbe:*

". . . feathers its cozy nest by night in the hull of a house.

"The pink and gold walls delicately enfold a feeling of warmth, the spotlight seems almost scented with orange; when the orchestra, at rare moments, stops playing, you can hear the tinkling of ice in buckets, and Skarjinsky's Russian accent evokes the quilted plush of a Slav cabaret."

December 4, 1941

The Chez Carrère, in the rue Pierre Charron, attracted rich French customers who preferred to avoid the occupation forces:

"The setting is that of a sumptuous eighteenth-century hotel. A large room with high, vaulted, aristocratic windows. Chandeliers hang from the ceiling. About fifty or so small tables, which are always reserved in advance. . . . What used to be called 'Paris Society,' and which, in spite of what they say, has not entirely disappeared, still meets here. Nods of recognition and friendship are exchanged from table to table. It is not like being in a public place, among a crowd of strangers, but more like attending a social evening that some wealthy patron has arranged for your personal distraction."

L'ILLUSTRATION,
January 3–10, 1942

In Montmartre, night clubs were everywhere filled. A woman on the staff of *La Gerbe* went with an escort to several night clubs shortly after the Germans arrived in Paris. She noted:

"At La Roseraie, there was apparently no room. Even so, we managed to get some seats. . . .

"At the Paradis, we were perched on high stools at the end of a narrow corridor of arms and legs. A violin surged out of the darkness. Everyone in the room sang the refrain of a sentimental waltz. . . . Uniforms everywhere, dignified bearing, immaculate dress. A blonde at every table. A neon sign lit up the smoky atmosphere. The 'girls' went off into the wings. Then suddenly, down from the stage onto the dance floor, a cascade of frills. A strip-tease show, featuring every shape and color.

"At Eve, we groped our way into a dark cellar, heads dimly outlined . . . A voice came from nowhere: 'Seats, madame? Only at the bar. . . .' "

July 18, 1940

At the Corsaire, according to *La Révolution nationale:*

"You had to grapple for places. And you got hit and shouted at."

June 7, 1942

"Singing acts" were in demand everywhere. A contributor to *Les Nouveaux Temps* explained why:

" 'Singing acts' have never been so popular as now. In music halls, cabarets and night clubs, they're as much the rage as they were at the height of the café-concerts. . . .

"Is this song revival, a typically French genre, to be welcomed? Unfortunately, the stupidity of the present songs is equalled only by their vulgarity. 'Leave me . . . Come back to me . . . Don't leave me . . . Take me . . . I want you,' moan the stars erotically. These slobbering ghouls are accompanied by soupy, outdated melodies."

December 14, 1940

THE TRIALS AND TRIBULATIONS OF OCCUPIED PARIS

The métro

The same journalist who left Paris on June 12 after seeing a herd of cows wandering in the place de l'Alma (see p. 12) returned after an absence of about two years. What were his impressions?

As he left the Gare de Lyons:

"Scores of fellows, of all shapes and ages, offered you their strong arms, would pick up your luggage, and limping along in your tracks, would cart it along to your house. The price was arranged beforehand. It varied from between 50 and 100 francs for about 30 to 40 kilos, and according to distance.

"Then there was my dog. What was I to do with him? Terrified by the din, the wretched spaniel stood there trembling, while the crowd rushed around him. I hid him as best I could in my overcoat. My porter beside me, I plunged into the *métro.* The place was packed to bursting. We made our way slowly down tunnels, interrupted by stairs. With my dog under my arm, I passed a notice saying 'Animals Forbidden in the *Métro.*' Then the porter went down a passage marked 'Exit only. Entry forbidden' in order to get onto the platform. Well, I was back in Paris all right!

"In the *métro,* I straightaway made contact with the new life of the capital. . . . I stared openmouthed at the crowd of which I was shortly to become a part. The first thing that struck me was how much better they looked than the people in Lyons or Marseilles. I suspected that their diet contained nutritive fats from the meadows of Normandy and Brittany. They looked well, too, because the women still seemed attractive, and though it was early, they all had on a spot of make-up, without which no Parisian woman is truly herself. . . . Among the men, there were a few officers from the army of occupation, . . . businessmen with bulging brief cases, their noses buried in their papers. At each stop, about fifteen more passengers piled in, and added themselves to the already congested mass of humanity. I hung on to a strap, to find there was only room for one of my feet on the floor. . . . Finally, I reached the place Clemenceau —right in the middle of the Champs-Élysées. . . . The place appeared not to have changed. The newspaper seller was in his stand, the man in the cigar store stamped my ration card for two packs of cigarettes every ten days, the waiter in the bistro on the corner gave me a cheery 'good morning' and started telling me his war experiences, the woman in the post office recognized my signature without consulting her files, and said, without looking up: 'You're back then? We were wondering what had become of you.' "[32]

It is hard to imagine how important the *métro* was at that time in Paris life, because there was practically no other means of transportation. New passengers had joined the regulars. People who had never gone out except in their own car or in a taxi became familiar now with a means of transportation they had never known before and which, in most cases, they found extremely disagreeable.

This is what a contributor to *Aujourd'hui* had to say on the subject:

"It was midday, and a crazed mass of humanity streamed past me as I went down to the Orléans-Clignancourt line. Every step I took, I got an umbrella in my legs, a parcel in my stomach, elbows in my ribs, and tense, angry faces were thrust into mine, so close, I had to draw away. All around was an atmosphere of stale air, warm breath, boiled cabbage and a curious mustiness; and silence, too—the silence of bodies locked in deadly combat, a dangerous silence, with fluctuating moods, in which one shout, breaking the tension, could provoke a storm.

"A young woman suddenly found herself in my arms.

" 'You!'

" 'You?'

" 'It's appalling. You can see for yourself. And every morning it's the same. It's like the Gadarene swine. The survival of the fittest. They literally trample on you. Look at my hat, and look! There . . . near my eye. That's where a suitcase caught me. And do you suppose the man so much as apologized?'

" 'I don't suppose so for a moment.'

" 'You can laugh! You're impossible. I tell you these people are ruffians, and all you do is laugh!' "

November 24, 1940

But the people who went by *métro* regularly soon got used to it:

"People do their nails in the *métro*," noted the editor of *France-Europe*. "The other day, a young man, with a pleasantly ironical expression, stared hard at a girl who was busily at work on her nails, and pulled a toothbrush out of his pocket. 'Why not make a thorough job of it?' he asked. Yesterday, the man sitting next to me treated me to the smell of the ripe Camembert he had in his hand, all the way from Étoile to Châtelet. I wanted to ask him where he had got it from. The odor was strong, and so was my desire to sample it. . . .

"Just now, again in the *métro* (it's becoming an obsession), a young married couple were starting their honeymoon. She had on a white dress and he had a gardenia in his buttonhole; and, obviously longing to be 'alone at last,' they were poking and teasing each other, with everybody watching them."

July 26, 1944

The last *métro* left at 11 P.M. The curfew was fixed at midnight, and if you missed it, you risked spending the night in a police station. Parisians soon adapted themselves to this. As Edmond Dubois wrote:

"Nobody invites you to dinner at 8:30 P.M. No, they definitely state: 'Be there at 8 o'clock sharp. You'll have to leave at 10:40 P.M. to catch the last *métro;* that way we'll have time to chat.' Shows close at 10:30 P.M., and if something happens to make them a few minutes late, the doormen quite often shout to the people swarming around the cloakrooms: 'Anyone who has to change trains, hurry up! Anyone going direct, let them in front. Hurry, hurry, it's twelve minutes to eleven!' In fact, everyone knows to the last minute what time his last connection goes from the station nearest the movie house or theater."[33]

Of course, there were always some who were late. One of them left a movie one October evening and looked at his watch—11:10 P.M. Disaster! Let him describe his superb performance himself:

"All around me, couples, arriving late, broke into a trot for the *métro* entrance, which was indicated by the feeble glimmer of a masked lamp.

" 'Will we, or won't we?' someone joked.

"I followed the rush, elbows tucked in, knees jerking obediently. The dread of spending the night in a police station under the strict eye of those guardians of the peace, inspired me to make an attempt on the world record. I forged ahead lithely, thrusting my way through the cold night air, as if I were part of it, like a whistling wind. I reached the pavement, stumbled, recovered, and staggered on, limping with my left foot.

"As I shot by, a policeman roared:

" 'Hurry up!'

"A newspaper seller murmured: 'What a business!'

"At last I was at the brightly lit entrance that led down below ground. Flushed and breathless, I bounded down the stairs with a crowd of night birds pattering behind me. The collector nervously punched my ticket:

" 'You'll just make it!'

"The brightness of those passages in the Concorde *métro*—like pure, gleaming intestines! An underground Arabian nights, with white canals, fiery red posters and cathedral echoes. A solid crowd flowed down them: men with paunches, with bowler hats jammed down on the backs of their heads, with scarlet faces, jogged along, gasping:

" 'Hurry, Mathilde, hurry!'

"And Mathilde, swathed in quivering furs, and made up to the eyes, her veil streaming in the wind, would hurry after them. Stately old ladies, their knees up and bottoms out, galloped along frenziedly. Young men, in well-cut suits and smart ties, passed them with long raking strides. Young girls, with radiant faces and coats flapping, skipped along, their heels ringing out like castanets. And everyone was laughing, asking questions, and joking in short, jerky gasps. The fatal barrier was open. I crossed in a dead heat with a distinguished gentleman with a snowy white mustache. He turned to me:

" 'We made it,' he said, as though we were members of some famous team.

"Then the train arrived, its yellow windows rattling. It was packed to the brim. But stomachs contracted, posteriors yielded, shoulders gave, arms went sideways, necks stretched, to let in another mouthful of passengers. The doors slid to with a bang, just behind me, and this human salad, tossed between four walls, shot through the dark to other destinations. I glanced to left and right at the solid mass of sweating brows, glazed looks, grinning mouths and dented hats. Every face was beaming good-naturedly. Everyone was smiling. This congealed slab of men and women was bubbling with a kind of end-of-semester gaiety. Face to face, stomach to stomach, people were talking away: 'To think there are some who never made the barrier' . . . 'I'm too old for this sort of thing' . . . I was watching you running, Nenette, you're definitely improving!' "

AUJOURD'HUI,
October 8, 1940

Cabs and bicycle-taxis

Old cab-horses came out of retirement, and with them, old-fashioned carriages and their drivers in the famous surcoat and traditional bowler hat. They had few customers, the horses jogged along painfully slow, and the fares were high, (a ride cost between 100 and 200 francs according to distance).

On the other hand, bicycle-taxis had a great success, and Parisians soon began to use them, especially women. They consisted of a bicycle or tandem, which was attached to a box suspended on two rubberized wheels. Inside the box, there was a seat with cushions on it. On the back of the vehicle was its name. As *L'Illustration* wrote:

"If you ask the men who pull these trailers around all day, they'll tell you that in spite of the high fares their company offices are inundated with bookings, even for the smallest journeys. Actresses have to be driven home at night after the last *métro,* and Paris is swarming with little red, blue and yellow boxes, like brand-new toys on strings, taking smartly dressed, well-to-do women around the stores. With their dresses gripped firmly between their knees, and their handbags beside them, they look as though they are being taken for a row by sturdy oarsmen with glistening bodies. . . . 'I'm not heavy,' they say sweetly and encouragingly, sitting on the extreme edge of the seat, and hoping to seem lighter . . . Most of them select drivers for their willingness and physique; others like to change around:

" 'I must have a blue one, to go with my dress.'

" 'Don't send me No. 10 again. He drives like a madman.' "

September 19, 1942

But nothing could compete in popularity with the bicycle. Here is Edmond Dubois again:

"The entire city is pedaling round, from nuns, going out to buy food or to make house-to-house collections, to respectable magistrates. People of all ages and conditions can be seen astride bicycles, leaping onto their saddles with varying degrees of agility, gripping the handle bars with varying degrees of athleticism. The city is dotted with open-air bicycle garages; people queue up at puncture-repair shops; spare parts are snapped up; and the oddest getups are worn by these would-be athletes.

"On the female side, housewives do their shopping rounds with baskets and saddlebags on their carriers for possible purchases, mothers carry their children on special seats, and there's always a crowd of women following the pack as best they can. Finally, there is the well-dressed woman who cycles because it's the smart thing, because it's madly Paris 1942. Her clothes are ludicrously impractical, and every time the wind blows her skirts up, she has to brush them modestly down again! This is the very moment that another blast of air plucks at her hat which is, according to the fashion, tall, large and flimsy. As she needs at least one hand on the handle bars, the lovely cyclist is faced with an agonizing choice: shall she keep her skirt down, or her hat on? Passers-by relish her dilemma. To make matters worse, there is usually a Pekingese or wire-haired fox terrier in a special basket over the front or rear wheel, which adds to its mistress' confusion by barking or jumping out. A delightful comedy that is constantly being acted out, in which the women of Paris handle their leading parts with inexhaustible skill and vivacity."[34]

The battle against the cold

After settling the question of locomotion with their usual grace, the women of Paris were confronted with another and more formidable problem: the cold. *L'Illustration* explained how they managed:

"Owing to the severe winter, smart women have wrapped themselves around with flannel, felt, fur and wool, like fountains in public gardens protected against frost. Everyone is drawing heavily on winter sports-clothes. Multicolored socks sprout from heavy climbing shoes. . . . In lecture rooms, only professors are still wearing gowns. Girl students sit there in skiing jackets and trousers. When classes are over, they slip on huge overcoats with high collars, which almost reach up to their tiny hats.

"Since it is not rationed, fur is greatly in demand. The skins of incredible beasts are made up into checks and stripes: cats—even dogs—and countless horses (some of the unusual shades indicate circus origins) go to make up this cubist menagerie. Many women who go by, huddled in sheepskins, look like ancient priests: their legs are thrust into boots or gaiters, and their heads fashionably garnished with flowers; they carry bags with slings, and lean on their long umbrellas as if they were alpine walking-sticks."

February 28, 1942

The winter of 1940–41, the first winter of the occupation, was particularly severe. A curious article in *L'Illustration* revealed the cunning and ingenuity with which Parisians fought back:

"These days, idle people find the best answer is to stay in bed, wearing a pair of fur gloves, a turtle-necked sweater, even a nightcap, which fashionable shops are already recommending. Those who have some definite job to do, count three and bravely take the plunge into the room, as into an icy swimming pool.

"To be effective, a cold bath must be followed by some vigorous contrast; the cheapest way to warm the body—and probably the fingers and ears, too—is by walking.

"The entire family, seeing they will only freeze if they remain in the charm and intimacy of home life, jump at the slightest excuse for leaving their unfriendly houses. From the Étoile to the Bastille, from Montmartre to Montparnasse, they march briskly, their collars turned up, until they're so tired they have to slow down. . . . Then they begin to shiver because their clothes are too light; so far they have only dared to draw on their sensible skiing clothes for heavy shoes and balaklava helmets. Their self-respect freezes at the extremities. . . .

"Sunday is the crucial day: children whine in the house,

and feel out of place in cafés. The Sunday walk, which used to end at the movies and museums, now winds up on a bench in a *métro* station, deep down in the fetid earth. Some churches which, till quite recently, were heated, used to make good stopping places: many people discovered a passion for archaeology, and a tireless devotion to some obscure saint, whose effigy was fanned by gentle blasts of warm air. But this wave of piety disappeared with the last sack of anthracite.

"Why aren't post offices open on Sundays?

"Post offices. That's something to fall back on when you've an excuse for a two-hour wait . . . Who cares if the seats are hard, and the door keeps opening; you surely wouldn't prefer the tax offices; though even these have their adherents, who claim that the waste of time is more than compensated for by the presence of stoves.

"Some people patronize hospitals, hothouses in the Museum, and monkey houses in the zoo. Some are regulars in banks, sit next to customers on benches and pretend to hold numbered discs. In this fashion, a day passes, out of the north wind. Public ingenuity is boundless."

L'ILLUSTRATION,
January 25, 1941

Rationing and queues

To this misery was added another, which was harder to contend with. Everything to do with daily life—food, clothes, shoes, and so on—was rationed, and the population found itself under the rigid control of the municipal services. The papers were crammed with requests and complaints, and readers' letters of protest were backed up by virulent articles. The German censorship, which was strict on political and racial questions, gave the "occupied" press a free hand in pillorying the French administration for its failures and excesses. Journalists made good use of their opportunities. On several occasions, their campaigns were successful.

Later, the ill-will and apathy of some of the municipal services was interpreted as their way of "resisting" the occupation by subtly fomenting discontent and making the Germans appear responsible for the people's hardships.

On January 14, 1941—that is to say, at a time when the severity of the winter had reached its peak —*Aujourd'hui* drew this picture:

"What is it we see and hear all round us?

"In the *mairies,* working-class women and pregnant women are queuing up at the counters for their allowances. On the whole they are given rude and unhelpful attention by a grumbling and overworked staff who waste the women's time, and who resent giving them information. Mind you, it's the same in most offices."

The editor of *France-Europe* described a fairly typical scene in his diary:

"Do you know the rue Jacquemont? . . . It is famous among the people of Épignettes, Batignolles, Ternes and the Plaine Monceau ever since it became a branch of the seventeenth *arrondissement mairie.* It consists of a rather sordid-looking garage and store, where the local food office is quartered.

"Any responsible, good-natured French citizen who turns up at the rue Jacquemont, leaves three or four hours later with a snarl on his lips and loathing in his eyes, boiling with a destructive hatred of present-day France, her methods and the incorrigible, pernicious stupidity of her administration.

"My neighbor, an economical, farsighted, practical woman, made a careful mental note of an announcement that appeared in the papers this summer, to the effect that when the children returned to school this year they would all get some clogs.

"So, as well organized as ever, she followed the paper's advice and waited until September before applying on behalf of her three children. On about the fifteenth, hungry but hopeful, she went to the rue Jacquemont where, after waiting an hour . . . she was admitted to the second floor, the shoe department, only to be politely told: 'You'll have to come back, madame, we've run out of forms. . . .'

"A week before the schools reopened, the 'mother of a family loved and cherished by the state' went back again to the rue Jacquemont. The entire neighborhood was there, hoping to find the blessed forms; it was obviously too simple to issue them through cigar stores. . . .

"She waited two hours on the ground floor. After chasing furiously up some stairs, so as not to be left behind by the pack, she reached the clog department.

" 'Queue up for forms,' boomed a uniformed watchdog.

"Another half-hour wait.

"Finally she got her precious forms.

" 'Now fill them in.'

"There were three pens and two inkwells for sixty people.

"A three-quarters-of-an-hour wait.

"At last she was face to face with the clog official.

"Another half-hour wait, while previous customers were being interviewed. Then, when that was over:

" 'You've forgotten to put your children's date of birth on the applications. Go and complete them.'

"Another wait for the pens, just to add a word to each form.

"At last, everything was in order, and sentence was given:

" 'You should hear in about six weeks. If not, call by.' "

October 10, 1942

Les Nouveaux Temps, in its number of May 3, 1941, described the formalities a mechanic had to go through in order to apply for a supplementary soap ration:

"1. Go to the *mairie* and collect, after a wait, a special form.

"2. Once in possession of the form, go in person to the Chambre des Métiers, quai des Jemappes.

"3. At the Chambre des Métiers, you will be told to obtain:

(a) your registered trade certificate.

(b) the tax collector's receipt for payments of tax in 1939 (sic) and 1940, toward expenses of the above Chambre.

(c) a personal application to an equalization fund.

"4. Obtain the three above-mentioned documents.

"5. Return to the Chambre des Métiers with these documents, and have the form obtained from the *mairie* stamped.

"6. Return to the *mairie*."

After all this, the applicant was entitled to 250 grams of soap. When two months had elapsed, he would have to start all over again, because it was possible that in the meantime he might have changed his trade. . . .

The municipal services, for their part, counterattacked, arguing the stupidity and ill will of "recipients" who mislaid their coupons, or didn't know how long they were valid for. The office that issued shoes complained that people applying for them didn't give sufficient reason for their needs. In particular, they only occasionally filled in the blank space on these forms (and there were enough of them) reserved for "special circumstances."

Although sympathizing with their readers' complaints about this office, *Les Nouveaux Temps* informed them on February 19, 1941:

"We gladly offer a list of 'special circumstances' to anyone lacking, not only shoes, but imagination."

The result was somewhat curious and unexpected. About six weeks later, this item appeared in the same paper:

"Some ingenious rogues have made calls on people who applied for shoe coupons in order to make a 'check up.'

"On the pretext of coming to see if their applications were valid, they ransacked the apartment. Prewar sugar, tins worth their weight in gold, non-ersatz coffee, carefully saved soap—all vanished! The so-called inspector pocketed the lot and, in the bargain, apparently lectured them on the immorality of hoarding.

"Rumors of these house-to-house visits began to spread, and many people decided to cancel their applications for the coupons they needed. The Préfecture de la Seine had to publish an official announcement, affirming that no check had yet been made by its inspectors, and that if any were made, 'they would concern only those objects identical to the ones obtainable by coupons.' "

LES NOUVEAUX TEMPS,
March 23, 1941

Le Franciste, on June 23, 1941, drew this conclusion:

"In three weeks, we shall all be going around barefoot."

This did not occur—and why not, will be seen later.

Meanwhile, one citizen did not stop at merely commonplace protests. On June 1, 1941, *La France au travail* reported this incident:

"About 9 A.M., a man was seen walking along the avenue de Clichy wearing only a jacket, and no trousers or underwear. He was arrested and taken to the police station. . . . He wanted, he said, to demonstrate against the trouble he had in getting his clothing coupons from the local *mairie* —an attempt which, in the end, he had to give up. 'I only had one pair of trousers left,' he went on, 'and I put them on the window sill after cleaning them. They fell down into the street and someone walked off with them.' "

The "demonstrator" was sent to Sainte-Anne for a mental examination. I don't know what became of him afterwards.

The most typical—and soon the most familiar—

sight in occupied Paris, was undoubtedly that of people of all ages and sexes collecting together in a line, which got the name of "queue." *L'Illustration,* on August 9, 1941, devoted a fair-sized article to this phenomenon:

"These queues are definitely the curse of our age: originating outside certain empty shops, they then spread, for no apparent reason, to every branch of industry and commerce, including theaters, local government buildings, railroad stations and *mairies;* since then they have spread from cigar stores to candy stores and toy stores; children coming out of school line up outside a general store for a couple of marbles; and on hot Sundays, this summer, small fountains, in the heart of the Bois de Boulogne, attracted long lines of drinkers, a thing which was never seen before the war.

"Whether for food or amusement, paying taxes or smoking, every citizen has become used to lining up with a crowd of strangers who express themselves mainly by using their elbows. People do it automatically, sometimes not knowing what they are waiting for, and only because there's a crowd, so it must be something interesting! All it needs is for two passers-by to stop at a store window. In a few minutes, a crowd has piled up behind them, the pavement is blocked, and the police arrive on bicycles. It doesn't matter what is in the store—it goes. . . .

"In winter, these queues had the advantage of forming an endurance test, so that a number of shoppers were quickly eliminated. In summer, they were an utter waste of time. The pavement became a living room where women came with the latest local gossip or world news. . . . Sitting either in a circle or in line, according to the lie of the land or how well they knew each other, they passed judgment on newcomers as though they were in a hotel restaurant. . . . Just as in the old days they chose their friends, now they pick their street and their waiting companions, whose social class varies according to their district and the articles sought. There are upper-class queues and working-class queues. Some are composed of cooks, others of idlers. Some are utterly without soul and character, because they are made up of strangers from all corners of Paris.

"Even those moments of leisure that used to be devoted to a dozen and one useless shopping expeditions, now give women the chance to try out new shops, stumbled on in the course of their wanderings, and even if their cupboards are full, they derive intense excitement from obtaining a bar of candy or a few ounces of cheese."

The most important queues, of course, were the ones that formed outside foodstores. Housewives worked up a fever of indignation against their grocers and regarded them as deadly enemies.

A *La Gerbe* reporter who asked one of his women friends what she would do after the war when things were all right again, received the reply:

"Personally, I shall set fire to my grocer's store."

December 4, 1941

A minor government official told the same reporter:

"Every evening when I get home, I feel like punching my grocer and milkman on the jaw. That's no exaggeration. The swinishness and stupidity of these store people is fantastic. And when my wife, who spends her days queuing up and submitting to the rudeness of grocer's assistants and butcher's boys, argues about it, I see red. 'It won't do you any good,' she says. 'Better to keep in their good books. Otherwise you've had it.' "

LA GERBE,
November 13, 1941

The author of this article continued:

"Two minutes after I left my informant, I passed a large grocer's shop in Passy. There was a queue, of course, and this is what I heard. I don't know what it was all about, except that a distinguished-looking and polite old lady may have been so bold as to complain of bad service.

"*The grocer's boy*: 'Now look, lady, if you're not satisfied, it's all the same to me, you can push off! You can go elsewhere! Come on, hurry up now. Next please! Yes, lady, you can push off!'

"*The cashier's comment*: 'Stingy old cow, going on like that for fifty francs!' "

A similar welcome was given by the "turnip-queens." According to *France-Europe:*

"At one time a Frenchman was supposed to live in terror of his concierge. Now, it's the woman at the vegetable store. She might cut off his supplies! So he has to make himself small, and be very pleasant, almost humble. He wouldn't dream of making a fuss because he'd been given short weight, or because his carrots were rotten. In any case, all he'd get would be:

" 'You don't like them? Right, next.'

"The Turnip Queen gestures royally. She juggles with the

vegetables, and bundles them tyrannically into her customer's arms. Without wrapping them, of course.

"It is advisable when queuing, not to push too much.

" 'Now then! Silence in the ranks, or I'll stop serving.'

"Immediate silence. Nobody crosses his vegetable store owner these days."

November 26, 1943

To this essentially feminine picture, add one from *L'Illustration* of a specifically male queue, at a cigar store:

"You've no idea what smokers have to go through to get their rations until you've spent a day serving behind the counter at a cigar store. We went by accident to a small store in the Paris region, shortly before the half-hour queue, permitted by law, began to form. On the pavement opposite, a crowd, poised for the attack, was growing rapidly: several hundred customers exchanged looks of hatred and pushed each other as they nursed illusions of precedence; those who had been waiting a long time ganged up against latecomers who were abusing the regulations. Heated discussions broke out, harsh words were exchanged, and chests swelled importantly under medal ribbons.

"At last the assault began, and it was a wonder the store window didn't break. Police, who were hastily summoned, anchored their feet against the door and arched their backs. Then at the allotted hour—not a second later—and under pain of threats, the distribution began. Pressed against the store window like rare fish in an aquarium, the customers could be closely studied from inside. Their faces were lined with worry and envy, and even when standing still they pushed each other. Suspecting favoritism, their eyes never once left the assistant's hands. One by one, they made their way into the store, trying to avoid the pressure of backs, shoulders and bellies, and emerging with unbuttoned coats and ripped ties. Like birds smoothing down their feathers, each one instinctively readjusted his clothing.

"Then they left by another door, calm, proud and well-behaved, openly and deliberately lighting their cigarettes."

July 19, 1941

A word about the "cases" especially made for "collectors" of cigarette butts:

"There are some very pretty ones, in wood or in worked metal. They look very old-fashioned, like snuffboxes. Very good."

FRANCE-EUROPE,
November 12, 1942

Sundays

I complete this brief survey with a picture of a winter Sunday in occupied Paris:

"You've been looking forward to it all week. You've made plans. And there it is, a fresh, clear dawn. Stay in bed late? Don't forget, if you want to light the fire, you haven't cut any wood. So you'll have to take the ax and chop up some kindling wood. Too bad about the tenants downstairs. And, hey, go easy on the coal! Your stock won't last all winter. And now, of course, you're late. The butcher. It's your turn to queue up for once. Your wife has given you a shopping bag for 180 grams of meat. It slips into your waistcoat pocket. Lunch. You've been expecting a package from the country; it's late. Result: no butter with which to cook the meat. And when there is butter, you've no meat. Which only goes to show, complete happiness is not a thing of this world.

"Now where can you go? Some deep thinking. You could invite some friends. But you've nothing to give them to eat. Cakes and pastries ease the conversation along, cement friendships. But requests to 'bring your own sugar' dampen enthusiasm. The movies? You'll have to queue. Always a queue. Even for turnips. Now your wife's feet are frozen. Do we go out or not? We go out. What about a cup of something hot in a café? '*Viandox,** *tilleul,*** *verveine****?' Everyone makes a face. You settle for *viandox.* A quarter of an hour later: 'Funny, that stuff makes me feel sick.' You have an apéritif. It's six o'clock. Fifteen francs for a glass of red wine! You'd have done better to have it at home.

"And what's there to do in the evening? Always wondering what to do; it's exhausting! 'Look, for once we've got a fire lit; we might as well make use of it.' You go home, the fire's gone out. 'I won't light it again; we've got to save wood.' Supper won't take long. And after that—well, you can always go to bed."

FRANCE-EUROPE
December 3, 1943

* A meat extract.
** Lime tea.
*** Verbena tea.

THE BLACK MARKET

Meals and invitations

After seeing a Parisian busily enjoying his Sunday, here are some details of his weekday routine:

"At 7 A.M. his alarm clock goes off. He prepares to leave, eager to get to his office. He used to turn up as late as possible. But now the office is heated, whereas his apartment . . .

"Downstairs, the grocer is standing outside his store. Monsieur de Paris greets him politely. In the old days, it was the grocer who greeted him. The morning passes. The office boy invites his boss to take an apéritif. In the old days, it was the other way around. But now the office boy is making money by selling cigarettes from one office to another.

"In the restaurant, it is meat day. Monsieur de Paris orders his meal. 'Give me a piece with fat, and a bit of stale bread. It'll go further that way.' Before, he'd have called the manager if he had been served a scrap of gristle, or because the rolls weren't fresh. Times have changed.

"Six o'clock in the evening. He buys a paper, and reads it in the *métro.* He gets out at his station. A newspaper seller is standing outside, empty-handed. 'Any old papers,' she cries, 'I'll buy your old papers!' She hands over ten sous. Times change.

"Back home, Monsieur de Paris' small son is back from school. 'Daddy, be a friend and do my homework for me. I've got my monthly accounts to work out.' Monsieur de Paris' son is in the second-hand pen business."

FRANCE-EUROPE,
February 25, 1944

Now and again, occupied Parisians had to invite a few friends to dinner. A correspondent on *L'Illustration* was intrigued by these gestures of hospitality, and dedicated a long article in praise of hosts:

"Anyone who invites his friends to a meal these days is a hero embarking on a perilous journey, and probably a rash fool. He will have to resort to the dastardly trick of humbly begging a few coupons so that his dinner becomes a kind of mutual charity performance under the patronage of each guest. He will have to undertake a pseudo-analysis of the menu, which has already had him queuing up at various shops since the crack of dawn. The guests will want to know if the weights of the various foods correspond to what is in the various dishes, and whether the cook hasn't made a few grams of butter on the side. The most insistent will be the scatterbrains who, either genuinely or not, forgot their ration cards; the people who used to be called freeloaders, but now have the lucky excuse of saying they'll send their cards on by mail, and the greedy relations who consumed their entire rations in the early part of the month, and are now living off other people's meat."

November 9, 1940

His colleague on *Les Nouveaux Temps* was struck by a curious phenomenon:

"You may have noticed this fairly common phenomenon in Paris.

"Before the war, some of our women acquaintances were slender, sylphlike, Pre-Raphaelite, almost transparent; now they've become beefy housewives with red faces.

"Before the war, they lived on zwieback, a little grapefruit juice, and an occasional slice of chicken breast. Now they use up all their bread coupons, and complain when, on meatless evenings, they can't order 'a nice, rare' piece of steak.

"It's a disturbing paradox. . . . so we made a small investigation.

" 'It's purely nervousness,' Mme. X. told us. 'I've developed an appetite such as I never had before, merely at the thought that I can't eat as much as I want; I've put on eight kilos in three months.'

"Asked why she ate so much, Mlle. Z. answered:

" 'Sheer patriotism! I want to see this war through to the end, and be ready for the world of the future. There may be some hard times ahead, so I'm stocking up.' "

January 17, 1941

Another writer, working for *La Gerbe,* happened to be in a small café on the rue Lafayette:

"It was noon. The bar was packed. Five minutes earlier, there had been only a few thirsty gossipers sampling high-powered rumors and low-powered drinks. They were swept aside by crowds from nearby shops and offices, mostly women and young men. Two of the women, next to me, ordered *Viandox.* . . . Others were drinking a yellowish coffee . . . All of them opened their bags and took out small pieces of bread which they began to eat.

"I offered a drink to the women next to me. But they hesitated.

" 'It makes your head spin,' said one of them eventually.

"The other said: 'And besides, it might make you hungry.'

"They then took two more *Viandox.* So deciding to go the whole way, I offered them a couple of crackers. Then the first one said solemnly and contentedly, without so much as the flicker of a smile: 'Good lunch we had today.' "

November 13, 1941

Food supplies

The greatest preoccupation of all was food. It radically altered the way Parisians looked and thought:

"Eating, and, more important, eating well," wrote a contributor to *La Gerbe* in the twelfth month of the occupation, "is the theme song of Paris life. In the street, in the *métro,* in drawing rooms, in cafés, all you hear about is food: how to track down some skinny bird or anaemic lobster like an Indian scout; how to arrange a genuine prewar meal on the sly (don't breathe a word!). At the theater or movies, when there's an old play or movie with a huge banquet scene, the audience breaks into delirious cries of joy."

LA GERBE,
July 17, 1941

This state of affairs gave rise to an economic, social and pathological phenomenon. The oversimplified name of "black market" obscured its true nature and complex structure. As Edmond Dubois wrote in 1942:

"The black market has become a vast hidden power. It controls food, stationery, electric cables, trouser buttons and machine tools. It has replaced the official markets for the sale of suits, cigarettes and tires. It has interests in everything." [35]

Its very existence, and the rapid strides it made, proves that in spite of German requisitioning there was no shortage of goods. But the official price lists did not allow its members to make the profits they expected, so they began to sell their goods to consumers how and when they liked. It is worth noting, however, that if it had merely been a question of a few businessmen lining their pockets by exploiting the need of the leisure classes for comfort and luxury, this evil, while still existing, would have been kept within normal limits, so to speak. But to make it so common and wide-spread, its range of customers had to be extended to let in the middle classes and the "economically feeble." And to make this possible, these new customers had to be given the wherewithal to buy the goods. Now, since the wages of employees, workers and clerks were insufficient, there had to be found an additional source of income. And it was the black market itself that undertook to find it. Everyone, from the top to the bottom of the social scale, was in it—big and small, young and old.

The black market was organized, and began to operate fully, at about the beginning of November, 1940.

About this time, a contributor to *Les Nouveaux Temps* made an investigation into the subject that proved highly instructive:

" 'So where is the black market?'

" 'Everywhere and nowhere. It could be in the back room of a stationery store, or in a comfortable third-floor apartment in the boulevard Malhesherbes. One of its characteristics is that it not only doesn't advertise itself, but it actually avoids publicity. And in spite of these entirely non-commercial methods, customers keep pouring in.'

"Someone may whisper in your ear:

" 'You can get some butter tomorrow in a shed near the porte des Lilas.'

" 'What price?'

" 'Fifty-two francs a kilo.'

" 'In other words, twenty francs more than the official rate.'

" 'Do you want it or don't you?'

" 'Of course.'

" 'Well, then, go ahead.'

"Not far from the porte d'Ivry, a vegetable store owner was running around in small circles. On the recommendation of a mutual acquaintance, I introduced myself. His customers were squabbling over carrots, leeks, and, in particular, cabbages. That morning, they were very scarce.

"In spite of the chilly morning breeze, there were large beads of sweat on his forehead. He worked with fanatical speed, never stopping for a second. At about ten o'clock, when he had sold the last pound of turnips, he shut up shop. . . .

"We went into a large, badly lit room adjoining the store.

" 'So Dupont told you I had some fish. He was right. I'm expecting it any moment.'

" 'How do you manage to get it?'

" 'From the country. . . .'

"At about eleven, an S.N.C.F. truck pulled up.

" 'Fifty cases from the country for you today!' shouted the driver.

"In a few minutes, the cases, each weighing fifty kilos, were in the backroom of the shop.

"I decided to help the boss unpack them.

"Armed with a hammer and cold chisel, I pried off the slats one by one. Carrots and turnips appeared, and then I detected the unmistakable tang of brine. I laid the vegetables on a table and went on with my search. I soon found rows of mackerel tightly packed under a thin cloth.

"The boss was undoing a box, too. First he pulled out some bunches of leeks that he flung contemptuously into a basket. Then, with exaggerated care, he took out some pollack that had been slightly damaged by the lumps of ice packed around it, and laid them on the shelves of a cupboard.

Parisian night club offers entertainment in German.

28

Queue before a shop on the rue Lepic.

To avoid waiting in line, clients had to register and receive a number.

" 'There you are,' said my man, 'in the other forty-eight cases I haven't unpacked, there are more mackerel, pollack, John Dories, red mullet, angler fish, eels, whiting and sole . . .'

" 'Aren't you afraid of getting into trouble?'

" 'You don't think I'm stupid enough to dispose of it here?'

" 'Most of it'll go by basket to the customers' houses in a minute or two. . . .'

" 'And what price do you sell them for?'

"He shrugged his shoulders:

" 'You don't suppose I'm doing this for nothing, do you?'

"He began to get annoyed:

" 'I'm not hurting anyone; my customers don't object to the price. In fact, they curse me if I forget them.' "

LES NOUVEAUX TEMPS,
November 4 and 5, 1940

The "new elite" of the black market

What was this "new élite"? What section of society did the leading black marketeers come from? It is impossible to make any hard and fast rule. In the Halles, according to one journalist, a kind of "mafia" grew up:

"Deals are made in bistros, even before the bell rings for the market to open. Do you want rabbits or poultry? Go to such-and-such a café! Do you want butter or cheese? You'll find some at so-and-so's!

"It's the same for a piece of pork or lamb.

"Prices fluctuate at about twice the official rate. For instance, I was offered some genuine coffee at 90 francs a kilo, butter at 50, cheese at 40, oil at 60, pork at 40 francs, and so on. . . ."

LES NOUVEAUX TEMPS,
November 29, 1940

They were all professionals, proven experts in speculation who learned their trade well before the war. They were joined by "amateurs," most of whom quickly caught on to their new trade, and showed a push and initiative they might have concealed in less profitable spheres.

They ranged from pimps to sons of good families —and very good families, too.

Here are a few examples:

First, pimps:

I.

"Before the war, he already had his headquarters: a small bistro off a suburban main street. His office was the bar counter, a glass of red wine, and his inkwell. From here, he kept an eye on his girls who were on their beats, waiting for customers. He pocketed the profits.

"The war. A stroke of luck! He found a good hide-out. . . . He went on with the job. It did well.

"The armistice. He kept his head. He opened new branches and added new departments. He dealt in women, soap, meat and silk stockings. He had it all worked out. Now he goes to smart bars. He won't touch red wine now;

he drinks American cocktails. He sells gold, butter and coal. He's invited to smart houses. He's such a charming fellow, so clever. Now he wears a diamond ring, so he manicures his nails. He is respected and sought after. He has important contacts. He expects to be decorated."

FRANCE-EUROPE,
April 14, 1944

II.

"M. Nénesse enters a small bar near the Opéra. He walks heavily and carelessly on thick, creaking leather soles to his reserved table.

"The waiters bustle around him. After adjusting his gold watch and taking a Chesterfield from his gold cigarette case, weighing at least 300 grams, he questions the staff, who answer him respectfully.

"M. Nénesse is sure of himself. He talks in a loud voice. He is displeased. He was supposed to be meeting some people and he hates to be kept waiting. . . .

"Out of a bicycle-taxi steps either an important colleague or a client of this 1943 tycoon. The new arrival is of indeterminate age, and his cheeks hang down flabbily over his collar. His suit is expensively cut.

"In the abrupt tones that you used to hear everywhere in the underworld, the two men converse. The newcomer tears a corner off the paper tablecloth and writes some mysterious figures on it. It all has to do with 'boîtes bleues,' 'paquets verts,' and 'douze tonnes de purée.'* Finally, the fat man pulls a thick wad of 5,000-franc notes out of his inside pocket, and M. Nénesse stuffs them away without batting an eyelid.

* Underworld slang. Literally: "blue tins, green packets and twelve tons of purée" (for various commodities).

"The phone rings. It's for M. Nénesse. He doesn't bother to go up to the phone booth; he takes the long-distance call downstairs.

" 'The trucks from Belgium haven't turned up. And the tobacco—the cases won't be at the railroad station till tomorrow.'

"Everyone can hear, but what does it matter? M. Nénesse is outside the law.

"Two men sit down at his table. One of them, large and cheerful, has a strong southern accent and a penetrating voice. He has come from Dax, where he has just acquired three tons of foie gras, which he is prepared to let go for the modest sum of 1,800 francs a kilo. He makes out he is starting a foie gras monopoly (*sic*) with his brother. A huge concern, with a big future.

"Without hesitating or saying a word, M. Nénesse takes a thousand kilos. Others—smaller fry—come over to the table. One has a thousand pairs of men's shoes for sale. Another, fifty meters of prewar material. A third, five hectolitres of 45 per cent alcohol, and powder sachets for making Marseilles *pastis*.

"M. Nénesse leans back in his seat, discusses, orders, buys and refuses. All this is a sideline; it has nothing to do with his real business.

"Before the war, plain Nénesse was in the white slave trade. After the defeat, Monsieur Nénesse traded in meat, poultry and butter; because of the quality, and, especially because of the regularity of his deliveries, he became supplier to all the black-market restaurants in the Champs-Élysées and around the Bourse.

"Every day, this honest tradesman sells 300,000 francs' worth of goods, and collects a cool fifty per cent rake-off.

"Mme. Nénesse makes a spectacular entry. At one time, she used to sell her favors on the corner of the faubourg Montmartre and the big boulevards. Now, she has just come from the Hôtel Drouot, where she bought a delightful little Vlaminck for 80,000 francs to decorate the dining room of her Chatou villa."

FRANCE-EUROPE,
June 26, 1943

Secondly, sons of good families:

"A few days ago, I walked into a bar near the Champs-Élysées. A man came up to me and held out his hand. He turned out to be a childhood friend.

" 'What are you doing here?'

" 'I own this bar,' he answered.

" 'You do?'

"He came from a very good country family: his father's people were in business, his mother's were in law. Jesuit education. He was sneering away, with his gang of cigarette girls, white-jacketed waiters and pigtailed lackeys all around him, laughing out of his great pasty face, like a jackass.

" 'You know, there's only one thing that matters today: getting on. You've got to get on, no matter how. You've got to be prepared to do anything today. My father's factory? I'd close it down. . . . I sell a bit of everything. Do you want gasoline? Silk stockings? I have girls to bring in the customers, and a night club in Montmartre, among other things."

" 'And what do they think about you at home?'

"He shrugged his shoulders:

" 'They've become used to it. They had to. The main thing is to make money. I'm getting my sister, who used to study medicine, to manage the night club."

LA GERBE,
April 16, 1942

According to *Les Nouveaux Temps,* there was a woman in the lace trade who dealt in butter and cheese:

"Smart women used to go to her for their Venetian point or delicately embroidered tablecloths, and then they passed through to the back part of the store, where an assistant, smiling graciously, handed them a kilo of butter and four or five Camemberts.

"This is how she managed it. She owned some land in a nearby *département,* which was planted with beeches and poplars. She got permission to transport firewood, chopped up by her gardener, to her Paris house. Under the logs and branches, she hid slabs of butter and piles of Camemberts bought from local farms. And that was how she managed to 'satisfy' her customers."

November 5, 1940

There was also a black market in the lycées. This little story appeared in *La France au travail,* around November, 1940:

"One of my friend's sons, who is at the lycée, came home last night to his parents covered in sweat.

" 'Have you been working hard today?' his father asked him.

" 'I'll say I have! Look what I lugged back, all the way from the lycée!'

"And he proudly showed his parents an extremely heavy bag.

" 'It's yours for 1,000 francs,' he told his father.

" 'Eh?'

" 'A hundred cases of *pâté de campagne!* What a haul!'

" 'A friend got it for me. I owe him the money.'

" 'Where did your pal get it?'

" 'His father owns a canning factory.'

" 'That's a good one. Just look at the stuff.'

"His father weighed a few verdigris-covered tins in his hand.

" 'You've been palmed off with some old rubbish!'

" 'I'll keep the ten heaviest. I don't like the looks of the rest. Here's a hundred francs. And that's too much. You can give the others back.'

"The next day, his son went off to the lycée, humping his load. That night he came back cheerfully, without the bag.

" 'Did you give them back?' asked his father.

" 'You bet I did. I sold them to the others. There's corned beef tomorrow, if you want some.'"

LA GERBE,
November 29, 1940

Finally, the children "black marketeers":

"In schools, French children are given vitamins, sometimes in the form of candy, sometimes as cookies . . .

"Opinions differ about the vitaminized candy. But the vitaminized cookies are in great demand everywhere.

"An extremely brisk trade, a virtual black market, has been rapidly started in most Paris schools.

"Colette is short of pocket money, so she sells her vitaminized cookies. Two days' cookies equal a movie ticket. Here, as elsewhere, demand exceeds supply, and prices are rocketing.

"Monique trades hers for candy, and Dédé, a budding housewife, for soap. Irène, for lipstick. Geneviève and

Raymonde keep theirs and conscientiously digest them, while Josette goes home triumphantly every night with the proceeds of the day's barter."

LES NOUVEAUX TEMPS,
June 8, 1941

As time went by, the black market lost its somber aspect. By the end of the summer of 1943, it had spread, colorfully and in broad daylight, to the main boulevards.

"Two sisters," wrote one reporter, "standing a few yards apart, were selling mending cotton, elastic at 35 francs a meter, and unrationed thread.

"An easy-going policeman passed them every five minutes. The black market didn't worry him. His job was the traffic.

"A large group of customers gathered around. These sisters were earning more than a hundred francs a day, and this performance had been going on for over six months."

FRANCE-EUROPE,
June 26, 1943

Do you want candy officially reserved for J 3?*

"At one *métro* exit, there are some pleasant women who offer you genuine candy. As much as you like.

"You need coupons to buy notebooks. What? You're not still doing that? At the same *métro*, you can get as

* J 3 presumably refers to a rationing category for children only.

many notebooks as you like. In broad daylight. As for the tons of herrings, which are held up at the moment and that you get on coupons as soon as they've reached an advanced state of decomposition, they're a thing of the past. Smoked herrings have invaded Paris, and grace every table once or twice a week. At twelve francs each, you can dine royally. . . .

"Do you want thread? There's always some on sale outside the *métro*—for no coupons. Policemen even buy it for their wives. What about soap? Do you want some of these green tablets that you get so few of for your coupons? There's a woman here with a caseful. Ten francs each. You can buy them by the dozen if you like."

FRANCE-EUROPE,
April 21, 1944

To bring this instructive chapter to a close, I quote a short conversation between two houswives that was overheard by a reporter on the same paper:

" 'Well, Madame Dubois, have you been for your December coupons? You know, it's a different place now that the kids are back at school.'

" 'Yes, I know. But do you think I'm going to hang around for hours queuing, when I can get as many forged ones as I want for nothing?' "

December 31, 1943

MORALE

Bad temper and anonymous letters

An attempt will be made in this chapter to show how the morale of Parisians fluctuated during the occupation. Great care will be taken not to generalize. This morale was not the same thing in 1941 as it was in 1944. It did not apply similarly to both middle and working-classes. And in each social class a distinction must be drawn between the young and the old. Also, in dealing with the old, businessmen must not be confused with intellectuals; and with the young, workers must not be confused with non-workers.

This will become clear from the occupied press clippings I am about to quote.

"Has France lost her soul?" George Suarez, who became director of *Aujourd'hui* in December, 1940, asked this question in May of the following year. A few days later, one of his colleagues raised the subject again:

"It strikes me as particularly serious that a man, commenting daily on the political scene over a period of months, should have to ask this question."

He went on to confess his personal anxiety. What struck him was:

". . . how sad, worried and edgy the French people looked. In trains, in the streets and cafés, the wretched people stared at each other with mistrust and despair. Every word betrayed suspicion, envy and loathing."

Another journalist made a point of noting the "catty" words then in vogue:

"In a few days, listening to people going at each other, I enlarged my vocabulary of insults by several new words. The most violent expression of dislike was: 'Get away, *vitaminé*!'* and if you wanted to brand someone who dealt with the black market, you could spitefully call out '*Espèce de sans-carte!*' "**

FRANCE-EUROPE,
August 9, 1944

* Literally: "vitaminized," or "person full of vitamins."
** Literally: "card-less" person.

What was curious from the earliest days of the occupation, was the vast number of anonymous letters and denunciations. "Anonymous letters abound in Paris," wrote *La France au travail,* on August 26, 1940. Like the other occupied papers, it had good reason to complain, because they all received a vast correspondence that attacked them vigorously and unequivocally for their activities.

But there were also experts in special kinds of letters. From September, 1940, onward, you could hear people everywhere saying: "I'll tell the Kommandantur." To avoid the trouble of calling personally, you wrote a letter. As *Aujourd'hui* wrote on September 14, 1940:

"In Paris, there is a group of poor wretches who are determined to take it out on their fellow citizens. In the old days, you were threatened with the magistrate, the sheriff or the chief of police. These good souls now invoke the Kommandantur. The Kommandantur is the latest incarnation of the bogeyman."

And in the same paper, on January 14, 1941:

"The appalling flood of anonymous letters and denunciations increases daily. What has become of the kindly old France that was? You'd swear that every Frenchman regards his neighbor as an enemy to be gotten rid of."

One of his colleagues on *Les Nouveaux Temps,* in an article entitled "The Age of Denunciation," made a similar point:

"One of the depressing features of our time is the prevalence of spying. Too many of our contemporaries are revenging themselves on their present misfortunes by denouncing, on some trifling score, their enemies; and if they haven't got any enemies, they pick on their fellow workers, neighbors or concierges.

"It need hardly be mentioned that the authorities (German authorities presumably) receive, to their intense disgust, scores of letters of denunciation. It seems they flood in daily.

"And when these experts aren't writing to the authorities, and seeing they can't write to the President of the Republic, they write to the papers!"

December 23, 1940

Another characteristic of the period was the epidemic of "rumors." In fact, this was not a new phenomenon. The epidemic had already been current during the "phoney war." A team of skilled rumor mongers grew up. At that time, in particular, circumstances greatly favored their activities.

The "English Radio"

The biggest and most effective of these circumstances was undoubtedly the Gaullist propaganda from London. Ever since the first weeks of the occupation, it had exerted a powerful influence on Parisians, comforting and encouraging them.

It was listened to with equal avidity and attention by both the middle and working classes. A writer in *La Gerbe* had to admit this. He did so with a certain irony and cynicism that did not entirely conceal his uneasiness:

" 'The English radio!'

"Everyone stops talking immediately. We are ten at table, but we all break off our conversations. The only one who didn't hear is a young man who continues leaning over toward his neighbor and goes on talking. Our host, who had gotten up to adjust the dials on his set, calls him firmly to order.

" 'Now look here, it's time for the English radio.'

"The young man blushes and looks down at his plate. No further sound. The butler stands to attention. Gazing at the luminous dial, we wait for the voice of London.

"I look around at the other guests. A year ago, they had all run away. Each man for himself, and the devil take the hindmost. But today, they're the bravest of the brave. There they are—well-dined, sipping their liqueurs, digesting a black market leg of mutton, utterly fearless. They're heroes, you see; they're listening in to London!

"Change of scene:

"In a small café in Menilmontant, some men are talking at the bar. . . . Suddenly, one of them glances at the clock and goes over to the radio.

" 'May I?' he asks the proprietor, 'I'd like to get London.'

"All around him they pat each other on the back, exchange congratulations:

" 'Takes a lot to scare him!' "

LA GERBE,
August 21, 1941

Those who heard the broadcasts passed on the news to others, often giving it a personal twist. Everyone added a little and it grew and began to vary considerably as it went from version to version. On September 12, *La France au travail* denounced "the poison from London" which "is infecting Paris":

"In the innocent guise of backstairs gossip and barroom strategy, it works its way insidiously into the veins of the population, defenseless against rumors."

A few days later *Le Matin* wrote:

"The age we live in is, more than any other, favorable to the circulation of false reports and absurd rumors. There is a kind of snobbery, a climate of skepticism that makes it fashionable to distrust anything the papers say, though at one time our fellow countrymen blindly accepted news that originated from highly dangerous and scattered sources. Today, they refuse to trust a press that has recovered a very considerable freedom of thought, and is constrained only by natural exigencies arising from the occupation.

"There is also a snobbery about 'private information'; everyone wants to appear smarter than his neighbor, to know more, and have his own unofficial 'tips'. . . . Finally, there are the whisperers who, by grossly and progressively exaggerating a few small, isolated facts, end up by playing havoc with public opinion."

September 19, 1940

This referred to a rumor that was current in Paris in mid-September 1940, that the German authorities had ordered a general requisition of bicycles and bedlinen. The rumor originated from a few, isolated cases of men in German uniforms, going into hotels, demanding sheets, and going off with any bicycles they could find there. The German authorities issued a categoric denial, which they followed up with this comment:

"An army at war, like ours, always collects around it a number of unscrupulous persons of different nationalities who have their eyes on what is called 'the easy deal.' It happens everywhere and in every age."

Queues naturally provided fertile ground for rumor mongering.

"I know of one housewife," wrote a columnist in *La Gerbe,* "who is not deliberately vicious, but is a gossip. Her great joy in life is the long waits outside food stores. She has established close relations with the local housewives, and, all day long, from grocer to tripe store, from butcher to fish market, she burns with insatiable curiosity, acting as a sort of vehicle for every kind of confidence, which she greets with the religious fervor of a believer kneeling to receive the host."

And he concluded:

"Fired by the hope of a bunch of carrots, or a long-deserved pound of potatoes, the whole city gossips. As usual, it talks without thinking; it listens, swallows and regurgitates. Some 'news,' of the 'so I hear' or 'I have it for a fact' variety, is an insult to simple human reason."

LA GERBE,
July 10, 1941

Interviews, October, 1941

The same journalist conceded three months later, however, that there were some people who remained completely impervious—utterly indifferent—to any kind of "rumor" whatsoever. But these people seemed to be living in some kind of soundproof box, far from the madding crowd. The journalist, looking for copy, decided one day to hold some "October interviews"—that is, interviews with citizens of occupied Paris in October, 1941. I will quote two.

I.

"It was in a bistro near the Flea Market. I got into conversation with one of those jack-of-all-trades so common in Paris, and especially in that area. He wasn't too badly dressed, and had a pleasant round face—or rather, a billiard ball with a long walrus mustache served him for one.

"I asked him what he thought of Stalin.

" 'Who?' he said.

"I repeated the question:

" 'Stalin.'

"He shook his head.

" 'Don't know him.'

"Then he explained:

" 'Don't know him. I never go to the movies.'

" 'And Pétain?'

" 'Oh, Pétain . . .'

"A pause, and then, as though he were announcing some important news:

" 'Seems he's been made President of the Republic.'

" 'But there is no Republic now.'

" 'Eh?'

"He shrugged his shoulders.

" 'No Republic? No Republic? How'd we manage with no Republic?'

"He fell silent. He took a drink.

" 'Soon be winter,' said the proprietor.

" 'Yes,' I said, 'won't be much fun for the prisoners.'

" 'Prisoners?' he said, 'what prisoners?'

" 'The prisoners in Germany.'

" 'Oh yes,' he went on thoughtfully. 'Seems there's a lot of them.'

"Another pause. My companion reflected, emptied what was left in his glass down his throat, ordered another, and said fatalistically:

" 'Might just as well be there as here, eh?' "

II.

"In the place du Trocadéro, I ran into a friend, or rather, an acquaintance—someone I knew through friends. I couldn't exactly recall his name, but I remembered he had some important job in industry.

" 'I'm just back from a vacation,' he told me. 'I badly needed the rest, but all we did was to traipse back and forth from restaurant to hotel, from hotel to restaurant. I'm worn out, and so's my wife, but we ate enough for four people. Not four, really—more like ten.'

" 'What do you think of the situation?'

" 'I brought back some rabbits,' my companion went on, not listening to me. 'Alive, you know. Two of them. Now I've got to try and find them some food, some greens.'

" 'What about the situation in Russia?'

" 'That reminds me, I wanted to ask you if you'd keep all your old cabbage leaves. As we live so near, I could send my man over to fetch them; anything will do except potato peelings, because of course they're no good for rabbits.'

"I interrupted him once again:

" 'You've been to America, do you think the Americans . . . ?'

" 'Naturally, when they breed, I'll give you a baby one. Oh yes I will! Do you know, if the female's any good, I should get nine or ten rabbits every three or four months?'

"He was out of breath. I cut in again:

" 'What do you think of Stalin?'

"He stared at me, wide-eyed."

" 'Stalin? Stalin? The Bolshevik?'

" 'I know no other.'

"Then, in amazement:

" 'What on earth should I think of him?'

"I remembered my conversation in the Flea-Market bar.

" 'Soon be winter,' I said. 'Won't be much fun for the prisoners.'

"My friend shrugged his shoulders:

" 'Oh, they must be getting pretty used to it, poor bastards! You know, they get more tobacco than we do.'

" 'Lucky dogs,' I said, with a straight face.

"And he kept a straight face, too.

" 'Lucky dogs? You can say that again!' "

LA GERBE,
October 9, 1941

In society

Now a short, idyllic picture from *Le Cri du peuple,* January, 1942:

"It's a small café and cigarette store in the sixteenth *arrondissement,* in a fashionable quarter of Auteuil. To be perfectly honest, it's what commonly used to be called a bistro, which is used in the day by truck drivers and local businessmen. But after dusk, elegant figures meet and disperse on the pavement in front of its blue door.

"Elaborate greetings, kissing of hands, all the polite conventions are observed. But what are these people doing there? It's quite simple: they've come to get their cigarette ration. . . .

"Doctors, writers, dramatists, lawyers, poets, painters and actors from the neighboring streets are registered there for their cigarettes. Some met up again in the bistro by chance; others struck up an acquaintance, made conversation over an apéritif, or, more often, an ordinary glass of wine; and they got into the habit of meeting there on a particular day at the same time. And then, before they realized it, it became a daily meeting place. Over its humble zinc counter, ideas for novels, plays and paintings are roughed out, collaborations born. A composer found his librettist there, and a poet—how lucky!—his publisher. You can pick up tips about getting food and how to cook it. Romances begin here; one has already ended in marriage. On some evenings, a well-known personality, though she doesn't live in the district, comes and delights the customers with her witty repartee, and is easily persuaded to sing a few of her successes. Like sensible people, they enjoy themselves placidly, quietly and soberly."

January 14, 1942

There was even a journalist of the "occupied" press who offered "recipes for happiness" to the would-be detached—that is, people who were world-weary and sought an ivory tower that promised complete security. This was in January, 1941.

"The papers are full of 'economical' recipes for making simple meals, but they seldom publish recipes for happiness.

"All you have to do is take the world and study it. If it seems too large, too cumbersome for your modest apartment, just take a bit of it—the bit nearest you, nearest your heart, your street, your village, your house. Wars come and go, Europe may collapse and recover before your very eyes, but there will always be white pigeons flying over Paris and perching on your window sill. The trees in your street, or along the highways, even when somberly veiled in rain or fringed with ice, are always storing up their warm, scented sap for the spring. . . ."

AUJOURD'HUI,
January 8, 1941

In addition to the "passive-detached" or contemplatives, there were the "active-detached": those who tried to show, through their deeds, that they wished to close their eyes to all that was going on around them by finding distractions that suited their personal tastes.

Thus "society women," or, at least, those who thought they were, spent their days in dress shops or drawing rooms, having tea, or playing bridge. During the summer of 1942, as Edmond Dubois recalled:

". . . They appeared in such a galaxy of printed dresses and garish hats that a famous designer, one of the undisputed arbiters of fashion, exclaimed: 'Women are mad! I'll bring them back to their senses this winter. I'll damn well stick them in black. That'll show them.' "[36]

Detective stories and poetry

The theater was very popular. Most of them played to full houses. But above all, people read. They had never read so much before. What did occupied Paris read?

A journalist took a walk around the bookstalls on the quays in order to find out. This is what he discovered:

"Parisians have taken a firm stand; no more love stories . . . On the contrary, they are greedy for detective stories, which are harder and harder to find second hand.

" 'It's not so much that they like crime,' " said an old bookseller who had been in the trade all his life, 'but they're bored stiff. . . . Detective stories keep them amused, give them a kick, you might say.' "

"As for other books, it's impossible to find anywhere on the quays a French-German dictionary or a book on 'German Self-Taught.' They've sold like hot cakes."

LA FRANCE AU TRAVAIL,
June 12, 1941

In 1941, the literary critic of the *Nouvelle Revue Française,* noticed a marked revival of poetry. He wrote:

"This year has witnessed an enormous blossoming of poetry in France, and our national genius will never have seemed so lively and varied."

September 1, 1941

About the same time, the following year, he wondered:

"Only from statistics supplied by the printers can we determine if the number of books, broadsheets and magazines devoted to poetry in 1942 is greater than that published in a similar period of time before the war; or if the present-day poetry movement seems so important to us because of its quantity, if not its quality, and because new prose works, which tend to distract our attention from poetry, have become more and more rare?"

N. R. F.,
October 1, 1942

A journalist on *La Jeunesse,* who ran the "Poetry" section, was more explicit:

"Every day there appear more and more supposed poetry booklets, and a vast number of broadsheets and pseudo-magazines that obstinately clamor to be regarded as poetry . . .

"Any dreary old bookworm, any idiot hawking his lack of talent around the so-called literary cafés of Montparnasse and the boulevard Saint-Germain, the Deux Magots and Flore, seems to think he's a genius, a superman of poetry, a prophet, with Eluard, Breton and Aragon as his gods, and floods the market with his own unsaleable (and unsold) effusions which, printed at his own expense, are more ludicrous than the feeblest efforts of a Prudhomme who thinks he's Corneille."

July 5, 1942

Only "mediocrities and babblers," to quote the words of *La Jeunesse,* which gave considerable space to literature, admired the work of Paul Eluard. The poet and his admirers were sternly warned:

"At a time when France has suffered great hardships and is trying to recover herself, the nauseating senilities that made our literature a laughingstock for a generation, are finished and done with. We wish to inform Paul Eluard and his friends and admirers, if they haven't yet realized it, that the game is up. No, young people won't be taken for a ride again."

LA JEUNESSE,
February 15, 1942

But it was his publisher, Gaston Gallimard, who, from the beginning of the occupation, was most savagely attacked:

"A band of crooks has been operating in French literature from 1905 to 1935 under their ringleader, Gallimard.

"A ringleader whose policy was not merely to line his purse, but to rot, poison and destroy. . . .

"Thirty years of mental cauterization! Thirty years of

slow moral decay! Thirty years of sly, degrading propaganda, in praise of anarchy, popular revolutions, 'anti' movements: antifascist, antinational, anti-everything. Thirty years of literary, spiritual and human nihilism! Gallimard and his gang have built the foundations of a noble 'scumocracy' . . . Gallimard, the poisoner of minds! Gallimard, the apostle of decay! Gallimard, the bandit chief! The youth of France spews you up!"

AU PILORI,
October 18, 1940

Even Drieu-la-Rochelle could not shield Gaston Gallimard from the volleys of the occupied press. On May 1, 1943, *France-Europe* wrote:

"What is this magazine trying to prove? That France is the prey of a drowsy conformity, like an old widow clinging pathetically on to the relics of the past. If so, it is certainly succeeding. A team of official journalists is hard at work on the insipid task of cramming its pages with opium and chloroform."

Hearing that the publisher had refused Rebatet's *Décombres* because of the "paper shortage," *Je suis Partout* observed sarcastically on February 19, 1943:

"Yet M. Gallimard easily arranged the paper for Aragon's huge book. The difference is, of course, political!"

Youth. The "Zazous"

The subject of Parisian youth from 1940–1944 is a complex one. Once again—and particularly with this topic—generalizations will be avoided, because it would be pointless to apply the same standards in every case. The subject, once broached, turned out to be enormous. It stretches from the "Hitlerian" lunatic, in boots and tie, hurling stones wrapped in newspaper through the windows of Jewish shops in the Champs-Élysées (see the following chapter), to the worker shot dead by German bullets while fighting against his country's oppressors (see, "Pour Qui Chanteront les Lendemains").

There were striking contrasts on the same intellectual level. A woman chemistry student worked as a porter (see *Le Franciste,* January 17, 1942).

And there was a student from the Polytechnic looking for someone to buy 5,000 packs of cigarettes at 80 francs a pack (see *Je suis Partout,* February 12, 1943).

The following sad tale, entitled "Disillusion," appeared in *La Gerbe* on August 16, 1940:

"A few days ago, we went to see 'Pasteur' at the Théâtre de la Madeleine. We felt that young people who hadn't seen it when it first appeared would appreciate this truly fine play.

"We therefore took the liberty of going and asking M. Sacha Guitry if he would give us a few seats for these young people. M. Guitry reserved the circle for us on the Thursday and Friday. We told various young people, all of whom replied: 'Yes, fine! We'll be there at a quarter to seven.'

"On Thursday, at a quarter to seven, we were there, all right. But at seven, there were only six of them, and at half past seven, there were still only eight.

"What's going on in the minds of French youth? Must we sadly conclude that if we had offered you the same seats for a cheap music hall, you'd have turned up a hundred strong?

"To think we believed in you!

"What's up with French youth these days?"

About the same time (approximately three weeks later), the following item appeared in *La France au travail*:

"What on earth do all these young men do, shuffling around the streets of Paris, with their wavy hair and their silk handkerchiefs, smirking and preening themselves?

"And what do they live on?

"Take a walk around Montmartre, or along the boulevard Saint-Michel, for instance, and you can see them by the hundreds."

September 14, 1940

The writer ought to have known about "young men" in Montmartre and what they lived on, unless, of course, he never lived in Paris until he got his job on *La France au travail;* though in the case of the Latin Quarter, the question was a fair one.

Here is a columnist writing in *La Jeunesse*:

"You can be sure that these curly headed sub-Tarzans, who go around parading their temperaments between Capoulade and Dupont at about three in the afternoon, will never understand the national revolution.

"Luckily, they are only a minority. That leaves the vacillators. They won't accept the new France until she makes a fresh start. They aren't very brave, but they'll do better when they've rejoined our ranks."

It concluded:

"The Latin Quarter must be won back from Jewish influence and Gaullist trickery."

LA JEUNESSE,
December 28, 1941

This "reconquest" was never made. Till the very end, these Latin Quarter "vacillators" refused their support to movements for moral and physical rearmament, organized for them by soul-savers in the Propaganda-Staffel. Yet there were many of them who, while remaining detached, adopted a non-conformist attitude, in the old Latin Quarter tradition of "shocking respectability" in any way they could think of. Clothing difficulties helped, and they delightedly welcomed the very severe winter of 1940–1941 as an excuse for wearing curious getups, which were at first greeted with surprise and amusement, but later set a fashion that took hold at the beginning of 1942. *L'Illustration* gave a detailed description:

"The men wear long jackets down to their thighs, dark, narrow trousers, heavy unpolished shoes, and either a cotton or a thick woollen tie. Being short of hair oil they smear salad oil on their hair, which is on the long side and hangs down over a soft collar attached in front by a horizontal tie pin. This getup is generally completed by a lumber jacket, which they show a great unwillingness to take off, even when it's soaking wet. They are most in their element when it's raining, and one of their favorite habits is trailing their feet through puddles, muddying their trousers and getting their thick, bushy hair soaking wet. The women, under their cheap furs, wear turtle-necked sweaters and very short, pleated skirts; their shoulders, exaggeratedly square, contrast with the men's, which are 'worn' sloping; their long hair hangs down the backs of their necks in spirals, their stockings are striped, their shoes flat and heavy, and they are armed with vast umbrellas that remain obstinately folded whatever the weather."

March 28, 1942

Paris gave them a nickname: "Zazou." Its linguistic origin has, as far as I know, never been definitely traced. (The diminutive, "Zazie," coined by one of our wittiest writers, is a later invention, dating from 1958.) Their rallying cry was "swing!"; it became a household word, and any self-respecting "Zazou" would repeat it tirelessly.

The circuitous route which they took to the Champs-Élysées remains, to me, a deep and insoluble mystery. As far as I can see, they did not make whirlwind raids, like Attila's huns, but used, rather, a system of slow infiltration, a kind of march on the Étoile, broken by halts, with particularly long ones at the Deux Magots and Flore.

Once they reached their destination, they pitched their tents, so to speak, within a well-defined radius, an occupied area in occupied territory, which became known as "Zazou" country. One writer, a patient geographer, described it in *La Gerbe*:

" 'Zazou' country consists of two café terraces, twenty small bars and about a hundred obscure dance halls.[37] Let's look in at the two terraces: the Pam-Pam and the Colisée.

"What a charming sight! Small boys, with delightful curls and their trousers at half-mast—the awkward age—and little girls with bare knees. It must be playtime. They keep leaping about on one foot with a hand raised. Is it some kind of hopscotch?

"Oh, no! When you get close, you see that these children are too old for that kind of game, much like aging women with too much make-up on. This is one of the soft-drink stands. Are these 'swing' boys abstemious? Oh, yes, because that's 'swing.' They adore harmless drinks: beer laced with grenadine, for instance! But it's 'swing,' too, to get drunk on half a bottle of gin in the 'family speakeasy,' playing Django Rheinhardt and Alex Combelle records.

"Leaving the blue and white model farm that makes them so delightful a setting, we go into another place, which is named after an ancient ruin. Here the 'swing' boys seem more serious. And the odd thing is, they seem to be the only customers! The terrace is 'swing,' the bar is 'swing,' the restaurant is 'swing.' 'Swing' money pours out of all these gentlemen's little pockets. What it is to be a 'Zazou'!"

June 4, 1942

The writer of this article imagined the "Zazous" were "supported by innocent parents." Perhaps they were—but not always. There is reason to believe their contacts with wild life on the Champs-Élysées inspired in them a distinct flair for black marketeering, which would have filled their pockets very quickly and conveniently.

The same writer also gave details of how the "Zazous" in the Champs-Élysées sector (Colisée division) spent their money:

"At a time when it is hard for a working man whose clothes are worn out to obtain coupons, or, even if he does have the coupons, to obtain a suit; when brides have to manage without white dresses—in times like these 'Zazous' can get everything they want. And their tastes are far from modest.

"While we are in mourning, they celebrate. While we dress as best we can, they choose the smartest 'Zazou' fashions with the insistence of a connoisseur in a black-market restaurant who demands an extra dash of madeira wine in his venison sauce.

"There is one solution: tailors should refuse to help them. But aren't we all 'swing'? Everyone encourages these crazy young fools: 'You come along with me. I've all the "Zazou" stuff you want.' Large shops hurry to lengthen their jackets and dress these little girls up like monkeys. Over there, in the window of a big store, surrounded by their precious scarves and ties, is an advertisement:

"A heart on the end of a pendulum. Up on top, a wig: YESTERDAY; on the right, nothing. TOMORROW; on the left, ZAZOU. TODAY; Zazou! Zazou! Zazou!"

YELLOW STAR AND SWASTIKA

All the perfumes of Arabia will not
sweeten this little hand. . . .
SHAKESPEARE, Macbeth, V, I

"Spontaneous" demonstrations

The agony suffered by the Jews in Paris during the occupation cannot be conveyed merely by assembling a few press clippings. A number of works on the subject have already been written. More will be. At least, one hopes so, because, human memory being short, there are things that must be constantly reiterated. In the following pages, only one aspect of this grim period will be dealt with: the wearing of yellow stars.

However, one or two points must first be brought to the reader's attention.

After the German Security Police had been established in Paris, there was included among its sections, as everywhere else, a Jewish one. Its head, S. S. Haupt-Sturmführer Dannecker, had complete control over the capital's Jewish population for more than two years. L. Poliakoff, author of *L'Étoile Jaune,* which is based on a vast quantity of first-hand material, described him as "tall and thin, the typical Nazi torturer. A violent and unscrupulous debauchee. He had personal control of several night clubs, which led to his removal in 1942. He was transferred to Bulgaria, once again as a 'Jewish specialist.' Afterwards, trace of him was lost."

In theory, he was supposed to work in permanent conjunction with the German ambassador, the Kommandostab in the Hôtel Majestic, and the "active" propaganda group from Propaganda-Staffel. In practice, he nearly always made his own decisions, obeying only instructions received from the central Dienställe in Berlin. For a while, he kept in the background, leaving Propaganda-Staffel "activists" to pave the way. These experts, who are not to be confused with the Presse-Gruppe experts, set to work immediately. Their final objective was the same as in all occupied countries: the total extermination of all

Jews, except for those few individuals who were considered "economically productive" ("Wirtschaftlich-wertvolle Juden"). But they worked by stages. It was vital to give the impression that anti-Jewish measures were in no way initiated by the Germans, so they pretended they were acting in accordance with the express wishes of the indigenous population (in this case, Parisians). The Propaganda-Staffel was to organize "spontaneous" anti-Jewish demonstrations. Presse-Gruppe "lecturers" distributed enormous numbers of news items and communiqués to the recently established newspapers. One of them, *Au Pilori,* had the job of recruiting a number of young Frenchmen for these projected demonstrations. Not much difficulty was found in recruiting a hundred or so young ne'er-do-wells, each of whom was given a complete uniform: dark shirt, boots, tie, beret, badge, leather gloves, belt, and so on. A house in the very heart of the Champs-Élysées was turned over to them. That was how the "Young Guards" began. In order that they could obtain some practice, they were posted in twos and threes at the entrances to Jewish stores. Their object was to stop customers from going in. This was about mid-July. The storekeepers became frightened. Non-Jews, afraid of being mistaken for Jewish colleagues, took precautions. This was the subject of an article in *Au Pilori,* on July 26, 1940, entitled "A Good Move."

"Some Paris storekeepers have put up notices on their storefronts, such as:

" 'French House, no Jews allowed.'

" 'This establishment no longer welcomes Israelites.'

"Others, more sagacious, had their notices printed in French and German, with the result that they attracted customers from the occupation forces."

At the same time, anti-Jewish posters were being stuck on walls. On July 31, M. Langeron was already noting "a new rash of anti-Jewish posters." [38] On August 3, a store window was smashed by a group of demonstrators. On the seventh, newsboys from *Au Pilori* broke into Jewish shops and overturned counters and display stands.

Until then, there had been only "skirmishes." The "major action" took place on the twentieth, when bewildered Parisians witnessed an unfamiliar sight. One fine summer afternoon, for two hours on end, the windows of Jewish stores on the Champs-Élysées were, one after another, quietly and methodically smashed. An American observer gave a detailed account of the operation in his book, which we have quoted from previously:

"I happened to be standing talking to a colleague on my office balcony overlooking the Champs-Élysées, when we heard shouts coming from the direction of the Étoile. An open, yellow car was passing down the almost deserted avenue; a young man, wearing some kind of uniform, was standing up in the back of it, shouting: 'Down with the Jews!'

"He left behind him what seemed like a wake of broken glass, because, as the car passed each dress store in the Champs-Élysées, a young man in uniform, stationed there, threw a brick, wrapped in a newspaper, through the store window. To my amazement, the huge windows of Cedric, Vanina, Annabel, Brunswick, Marie-Louise and Toutmain —a million franc's worth of glass—exploded into fragments on the pavement. Most—if not all—of these establishments were Jewish-owned, and had been reopened by their loyal French employees, who stood between the counters trembling and crying. Their work done, the uniformed young men went along the avenue to Number 36, the Young Front Headquarters,[39] and leaned out of the windows, laughing and jeering at the angry crowd that had gathered . . .

"I saw a German officer leave the Hotel Claridge, which had been converted into offices for the Germans, just as a brick smashed the next-door store window. The officer grabbed the culprit by the collar, but the latter pulled a card out of his pocket. I don't know what the card was, but I saw the officer glance at it and immediately release the prisoner."[40]

The occupying powers intervene

The operation went on the next day.[41] It seemed to have thoroughly satisfied the German authorities because they decided the time had come to intervene personally. Pretexts were easy to come by. Jewish businesses that had remained shut, their owners not having returned, were reopened "so as to insure work for the staff," and put under non-Jewish management. Immediately afterwards, the same measures were applied to businesses whose owners were present. Then it was the turn of Jewish residences, where art treasures, already placed under protective custody by the decree of July 15, (quoted on p. 33), were put at the disposal of the occupation authorities.

After Jewish possessions came the turn of the Jews themselves. The objective remained the same: to rid Paris of Jewish stock. Because of the census made in December, records existed of their numbers and composition.

They began with Jewish immigrants who had not yet acquired French nationality. *Paris-Midi* described what happened on May 14, 1941:

"For two days, the Paris ghetto has been in turmoil.

"In fact, yesterday evening, a number of foreign Jews were sent summonses, requesting them to be at a given place the following morning at seven for 'matters concerning them.'

"The brief note added: 'You are requested to bring a member of your family with you.' So yesterday, at seven, several thousand Jews met at the stated place: either at the Japy gymnasium, the Minimes barracks, the rue de la Grange-aux-Belles or the rue Edouard Pailleron.

"Some were laughing or joking, but their mirth soon vanished when they were told:

" 'All persons accompanying their relatives will be given a notice that they are requested to study carefully. They have three-quarters of an hour in which to make the short journey proposed and bring back the objects required.'

"On the paper was written: 'You will go immediately to your relative's house and bring him a blanket, a change of underwear, cutlery, a mess-tin, food for twenty-four hours, and so on. . . .'

"Everyone understood immediately. It was, at last, what

the French have so long wanted: the application of the law of October 4, 1940.

"Less than an hour afterwards, the 'relatives' came back with meager bundles that had been hastily put together. A few hysterical cries, one or two noisy remonstrances, and order was restored. Flanked by policemen and Republican guards, the Jews climbed into the buses and trucks of the Auxiliary Police. By 11 A.M. they were on the platforms of the Gare d'Austerlitz."

This description was accompanied by the following comment:

"Five thousand Jews left, five thousand Jews spent their first night in a concentration camp. Five thousand less parasites in the mighty city of Paris, which they had mortally infected. The first incision has been made; others will follow."

PARIS-MIDI,
May 15, 1941

The man who wrote these lines knew what he was saying.

So Paris was "rid" of her foreign Jews. The French Jews remained. According to the 1939 figures, there were, at the time, 300,000 Jews in Paris (or, at least, in the Paris area). Five thousand had just been eliminated. That left 295,000. Anyway, that was the estimate given by *Le Franciste,* which asked, about two months after the operation of May 14:

"When will someone decide to lock up these 295,000 foreigners?"

But it had not allowed for those who left in the June exodus and had not returned. It would seem that the number of Jews in the Paris area was about 200,000, of whom 110,000 were in Paris itself. In fact, the check made in November, 1941, established the number of Jews in Paris as 92,864 aged over fifteen, and 17,728 children between the ages of six and fifteen.

Before undertaking the total elimination of the Jewish population, which involved the two stages of internment and deportation, the German authorities decided to create a barrier that would visually and effectively distinguish Jews from non-Jews.

This was the aim of a decree issued by the Militärbefehlshaber on June 1, 1942, by which Jews were compelled to wear yellow stars, and which was to become effective as of the seventh of the same month.

The "active propaganda" group of the Propaganda-Staffel that was responsible for conditioning French public opinion and popularizing this measure, suggested to the French Ministry of Information that the cigarette ration should be withdrawn from Jews living in the occupied zone, in favor of French prisoners.

According to a report on the subject sent by the section to Dannecker, the ministry considered the idea "very astute from the psychological point of view, and valuable from the propaganda angle." [42]

However, nothing came of it.

How did the Jews react? On June 2, Zeitschel, an embassy adviser, wrote to Dannecker:

"It seems that the Jews are planning a huge propaganda march in the Champs-Élysées on the seventh of June. This would provide an opportunity for swiftly diverting the Jewish column to Drancy under military escort."

Three days later, on June 5, the Propaganda-Staffel sent this report to the German Security Police:

"According to reports coming in hourly, Gaullist and Communist circles are putting out enormous amounts of propaganda with the aim of fomenting trouble next Sunday. The directives issued are as follows: all Jews on the main boulevards wearing yellow stars are to be greeted with demonstrations of sympathy. . . . It is planned that non-Jewish Gaullists and Communists will circulate, wearing yellow stars which, instead of bearing the inscription 'Jew,' will display the names of French provinces."

The next day, the sixth, it gave these additional details:

"Gaullists and Communists will show their disapproval in the following manner:

"1. By wearing yellow flowers.

"2. By wearing yellow handkerchiefs in their breast pockets.

"3. By wearing Jewish stars made out of paper."[43]

A substantial report on the events of the actual day, Sunday, June 7, was sent to the German Security Police by the Propaganda-Staffel on June 10:

"With regard to the Jews, an order seemed to have been given by which all Jews were to turn up on the Sunday afternoon (June 7) in the main boulevards, between the place de la République and the Opéra. This order was obeyed: it was amazing to see how many Jews turned up in the stated place. . . . Groups of Jews strolled along the boulevards and sat down together in cafés and restaurants. Also, it was noticeable how many Jewish mothers were out with their babies and baby carriages, as a form of demonstration."[44]

A German police observer wrote this description:

"On Sunday, June 7, Jewish veterans of the 1914–1918 war were wearing all their medals, just above the Jewish star. The men were wandering around the streets, in most cases attracting little attention. The women, on the other hand, especially in the Goutte d'Or, Barbès, and la Chapelle districts, were talking away noisily, letting it be known that they were proud to be wearing their racial emblem."[45]

One of his colleagues noted that, in the eighth and ninth *arrondissements,* there were Jews present "wearing stars on their backs, sewn on at the level of their buttocks."

Parisians react

Contrary to the hopes of German propagandists, the majority of Parisians were revolted by the yellow star order. A good many former anti-Semites made no attempt to hide their disapproval. Generally speaking, the only people to applaud the move were the journalists of the "occupied" press, and the Déat, Doriot and Company "youth." A report from police headquarters mentioned that from "about 4:20 P.M. onward, a dozen or so persons, carrying a banner that displayed a horseshoe with a torch inside it (the badge of the Rassemblement National Populaire, founded by Déat) were passing through the boulevard de la Madeleine and the rue Royale, in the direction of the place de la Concorde, and denouncing the Jews. In a café on the boulevard des Capucines, they tried to stop a waiter serving Jewish customers, and on the boulevard de la Madeleine, members of the group struck a Jew who was wearing his badge and sitting outside the Brasserie Weber."

There were many Parisians who, not content with speaking their disapproval, wanted to show it actively. Here are a few isolated cases. There were many others.

On the seventh, a young girl of eighteen, a student from the École Alsacienne, was arrested in the boulevard St. Germain for carrying two cardboard posters on which were written: "bouddhiste" and "buddhist." She was then known as Mlle. Solange de Lipkowski. A little farther along the same street, a young woman painter of twenty-three, Mme. Madeleine Bonnaire, was arrested and taken to the St. Germain des Prés police station for having her coat decorated with a yellow star. "On the way there," said the police report, "Mme. Bonnaire rushed up to a group of a dozen German soldiers, and thumbed her nose at them."

The following day, June 8, Roland Borivant, twenty, a baker by trade, was walking around sporting a yellow star, while Henri Plard, a twenty-three-year-old student, decided to carry a yellow paper handkerchief in his breastpocket, with nothing written on it, but with the top part cut in the shape of a star.

On the tenth, two workers, Nicholas Rebora and Lazare Villeneuve, aged nineteen and twenty-two respectively, were seen displaying yellow stars. Tony Basset, a sixteen-year-old college student, decided to wear his with the inscription "Zulu," and Michel Ravet (a twenty-one-year-old business employee) had on his "Goï." On the eleventh, some of the "Zazous," (or at least their adherents), joined the movement. Michel Reyssat, a student, and Emile Augier, a Treasury employee, both had the inscription "swing" on their badges.

The women showed more imagination. Josèphe Cardin, a nineteen-year-old student, as well as having a yellow badge, fixed eight stars to her belt, with a letter on each one, spelling out the word "Victoire." Paulette Voisin, another nineteen-year-old student, wrote the figure "130" in the middle of her badge. What did it mean? A mystery . . . But Françoise Siefridt, twenty years old, another student, was more explicit. Hers read: "Papuan." Typists showed a preference for Christian names: Jenny Wion and Denise

Recouvrot, both twenty-one, embroidered their Christian names on yellow stars attached to their dresses. Paulette Pecoil, a twenty-two-year-old P.T.T. worker, had nothing on hers. But Simone Decise, a twenty-three-year-old stationer, made herself a yellow star disguised as a rose.

These were the "under twenty-five-year-olds." Now for their elders. Alice Courouble, a twenty-nine-year-old secretary, and Jean-Pierre Simonnet, a thirty-year-old electrician, wore ordinary yellow stars. Henri Muratet, a thirty-nine-year-old architect, wrote "Auvergnat" on his, and Marie Lang, a twenty-eight-year-old newspaper seller, tied a Jewish emblem to her dog's collar. Then there was Mme. Lemeunier, fifty-eight years old, without a profession, who appeared in the street wearing a yellow star with an embroidered cross on it. She was sent, with the others, to Drancy. They stayed there about three weeks. The *National-Populaire* wrote the following on the subject, under the heading "Protect the Race."

"In spite of the revulsion most French people feel for the Jews, there are still some very 'swing' young people who have become completely Jewified and who show their sympathy for them by wearing yellow stars. The government must separate these undesirables from the French people, and satisfy their wish to belong to the Jewish community by giving them full Israeli status, and treating them accordingly. In this way, they could benefit from any measures we may have to take in connection with the Jews."

June 20, 1943

Exceptions

The decree of June 1, 1942, provided for exceptions "in isolated cases, and under special circumstances, in the interests of the Reich."

Referring to this provision, Marshal Pétain wrote to F. de Brinon, on the following June 12:

"My attention has just been drawn to various aspects of the regrettable situation which will result (from the application of this decree) in certain French homes. . . . I am convinced that the German High Command realizes perfectly that some exceptions are indispensable; in any case, the text of the eighth decree provides for them. And I feel this is essential for just (*sic*) measures against the Jews to be understood and accepted by Frenchmen." This was why, in the Marshal's opinion, the Commissioner for Jewish Affairs should "quickly arrange for exceptional and individual measures, so as to deal with cases of special hardship which may be brought to our attention."

As a result of Brinon's overtures, the three exceptions the Marshal requested were granted. They concerned "wives of non-Jews" from good social backgrounds.

On June 18, there was a conference at the German Embassy at which were present the following: Abetz and his two colleagues—Minister Rahn and Dr. Zeitschel—on one side; and Oberg, who was supreme head of the German police in the occupied zone, his aide Dr. Knochen, and Sturmbannführer Hagen, who was responsible for enforcing the June 1 decree, on the other. When Oberg asked who the Jews were who were to be exempted "in the interests of the Reich," Abetz asked the favor for Bergson's widow (the great philosopher had died on January 4, 1941) and for the wives of two writers. One of these was identified by the single initial "J." The name of the other, Caulette, is, as far as I can see, unknown to French literature.[46]

A similar favor was granted to eight brokers or contractors, working for German commercial firms in Paris, and to fourteen "informers" (seven working at the Abwehrstelle, or German counterespionage service, six anti-Jewish policemen, and an agent in the German Security Police Information Service).

The colonel in charge of the Paris fire brigade, who requested the dispensation for twenty-eight Jewish N.C.O.'s and firemen under his command, was met with a flat refusal.

Finally, there is the strange case of Hauptsturmbannführer Joseph Wilberger (an Austrian, apparently) who had the job of buying various commodities in Paris for the Upper Danube Province. When he arrived, he got in touch with two "pure" Jews ("Volljuden"), who helped him very considerably. When the decree about the wearing of yellow stars came into force, he issued to them, on his own authority, certificates of exemption on forms which he had acquired from the office of a member of the embassy staff. According to a report by the head of the Anti-Jewish Bureau in Berlin:

"It is significant that Wilberger gave these certificates to the Jews on the occasion of one of their birthdays, commenting that it was the nicest present he could think of."

This was not all, the report said:

"Wilberger was also on intimate terms with a Frenchwoman . . . (a Jewess), thirty years younger than himself. He made her his secretary, and entrusted his business both to her and the two Jews."

This tender-hearted civil servant was eventually recalled and interned at Linz. I do not know what became of him in the end.

The persecution intensifies

Everything seemed to indicate that developments would not end there, and that the June 1 decree would be followed up. An article in the *Cri du peuple,* which was as bitterly anti-Semitic as *Au Pilori,* pointed the way:

"For some days, Israelites, with or without their yellow stars, have with their continual insolence provoked a number of incidents in respectable cafés, hotels and restaurants. The behavior of some of these Jews has been disgusting, and must not be tolerated. As a result, and in deference to the feelings of the owners of innumerable restaurants, café's, hotels and bars, the heads of the Paris region of the P.P.F. (the Parti Populaire Français, led by Doriot) has asked the trade union concerned to indicate, by arrangement with the relevant authorities, those establishments which may be patronized by Jews. Entry to all other establishments will be strictly barred to all Jews."

AU PILORI,
June 29, 1942

Ten days later, General Oberg signed the decree listing those establishments and public places that Jews were forbidden to enter:

1. Restaurants and eating places.
2. Cafés, tea shops and bars.
3. Theaters.
4. Movie houses.
5. Concert halls.
6. Music halls and other places of entertainment.
7. Public phone booths.
8. Markets and fairs.
9. Swimming pools and beaches.
10. Museums.
11. Libraries.
12. Exhibitions.
13. Castles, country houses of historic interest, or any other historic monument.
14. Sporting events, either as participants or spectators.
15. Racetracks and betting places.
16. Camping grounds.
17. Parks.

Le Petit Parisien, which published this text, made the following comment:

"For some time, too many Jews, especially young ones, have been flaunting their confounded insolence in public places, on café terraces and on racetracks. And when the decree about the compulsory wearing of yellow stars was issued, many of them arrogantly and ostentatiously flaunted their racial badges on café terraces, at sports grounds and other public places.

"It was the Jews who wanted the war. It was their evil-minded race that plunged the whole world into this terrible conflict. In view of this crime, the recent measures seem almost benevolent."

July 15, 1942

This was a hint that there might be further measures. In fact, on the same day there occurred that hideous raid which is commemorated by a plaque affixed to the front of the Vélodrome de Paris after the liberation:

JULY 16, 1942

THIRTY THOUSAND JEWS, MEN, WOMEN AND CHILDREN, VICTIMS OF RACIAL PERSECUTION, WERE ENCLOSED HERE BY ORDER OF THE NAZI OCCUPATION AUTHORITIES, THEN SPLIT UP, DEPORTED TO GERMANY, AND PUT IN EXTERMINATION CAMPS.

YOU ARE FREE! DO NOT FORGET!

"POUR QUI CHANTERONT LES LENDEMAINS?"

Beginnings of the Resistance

As early as July 8, 1940, only three weeks after the Germans had entered Paris, a well-meaning citizen, who introduced himself as "an average intellectual, and a teacher by profession," wrote in *La France au travail:*

"What I want to see is this present state of occupation, which we must put up with for some time to come, working out as satisfactorily as possible, both for you (*sic*) and for us. Now, though things have started well, it seems that certain individuals take exception to the good feelings that exist between the people and the occupying forces. Yesterday, a small crowd had gathered near a *métro* station, and some man of indeterminate profession began to harangue and incite his audience to revolt against the Germans. His arguments were ludicrous, or, I should say, non-existent. It is in the public interest that there should be no incidents, and that the population's attitude should be such that the Kommandantur should not be obliged to take Draconian measures. But if people listen to trouble-makers, things will quickly deteriorate. I can speak freely to you about this, because those to whom I refer are not Frenchmen but some kind of foreigners. God knows where they came from; we have foolishly sheltered them, and now they want to foment trouble instead of letting us live in dignity."

This kind of propaganda appeared in the most varied guises. One of the first—if not the very first—was on posters. The editor of the underground paper, *Valmy,* who crossed to England toward the end of 1941, recalled in *La France libre:*

"I was in Paris when the capital was occupied. No one had expected it. But on the fifth day of the occupation, the first shock over, I began to organize an early resistance group with some friends.

"We bought some rolls of paper in a shop, the kind you stick on windows for protection against air raids. We printed slogans on them. One went: 'A single foe—the invader'; this was taken up by the French radio—the real one—in London.

"Then again: 'The Nazi vacuum cleaner cleans the country in seconds.' And 'Liberty–Equality–Fraternity–Vive de Gaulle!' We went out ourselves and stuck these posters all over Paris and the suburbs—thousands of them. We stuck them under the very noses of the Germans, on the sides of bridges and on lampposts. We went one better; we translated them into German: Who is the finest Aryan in Europe? Dr. Goebbels. Who is the biggest plutocrat in Europe? Herman Goering. Who is the last tyrant in Europe? Adolf Hitler,' and we stuck them on cars belonging to the German army, in order to demoralize the occupants."

January 23, 1942

There was also the "scribbler's war" which infuriated one writer on *Les Nouveaux Temps:*

"It takes a brave man to chalk a few marks on a wall or on the inside of a public toilet on a pitch-black night.

"That's about the extent of most Frenchmen's courage. No wonder we finished up how we did.

"These sort of people are always ready for safe demonstrations.

"The same chalk sent 'Blum to the gallows,' and condemned the impetuous Colonel de la Rocque; all parties have their compulsive scribblers.

"The one thing they have in common is caution.

"That's something they share with their first cousins: the anonymous letter writers."

April 4, 1941

However, there were some "uncautious" people who didn't hesitate to show themselves—and ostentatiously, too. Here is a furious article on the subject, which appeared in *La France au travail:*

"A few idiots—though *a few* is putting it mildly—are trying to show off.

"And some, even more stupid if that is possible, are aping them.

"I come across them every day.

"Yesterday, it was a young ass wearing the Cross of Lorraine, the Gaullist badge, on his lapel. He seemed to be very pleased with his little game.

"Two days before, it was some fool in a large café near the Madeleine who insulted a young man for trying to sell him a postcard of Marshal Pétain in aid of the Winter Relief Fund."

January 1, 1941

The following curious incident was described by a reporter on *Aujourd'hui* on the twenty-eighth of December:

"I was reading an evening newspaper yesterday in the *métro,* Bastille and Concorde, when an aggressive young voice behind me said:

" 'You must be crazy to read the papers!'

"I acted shy, and pretended I couldn't hear, but the voice grew louder and more insistent, repeated its opinion, and even went so far as to ask a young woman to agree how stupid and credulous I was. This time I decided to ask for an explanation, so that at least I could plead extenuating circumstances.

" 'Excuse me,' I said, 'does it really worry you to see me reading this paper?'

"The man's voice hesitated a second. He was a young man—in fact, almost a child.

" 'Yes, it does,' he finally answered, 'because the papers are not free.'

" 'Whereas you, of course, are?'

" 'Well, I'm free not to read them,' he replied vigorously.

" 'I've no wish to stop you,' I said graciously.

"He fell silent. But he stared at me so angrily, with such melodramatic hatred, that if looks could kill, I believe you would now be attending my funeral."

A charming poet, a gentle and elegiac night bird, who succumbed to the wiles of *Aujourd'hui,* wrote on April 2, 1941:

"Today, whether we like it or not, the whole train of events favors aspirations and impulses towards eloquence and volubility, whether written or spoken. It is a truism that, deep down inside him, man prefers words to silence. Many people deplore reserve because they don't wish to appear ignorant. So they keep going and throw discretion to the winds.

"Silence is a weapon, and possibly the most powerful of all. It is the night light of speech, a disguise, a protection. . . . In this dramatic age, we must learn to be sparing in our use of words, and betray neither ourselves nor anyone else."

Communist action

We now turn to another kind of propaganda: that issued by the Communist party.

In mentioning the party's attitude toward the occupation, it has become common to say that this attitude changed only from June 22, 1941, onward (the day Germany went to war with the Soviet Union) and that until then, it never showed any signs of hostility.

An examination of the "occupied" press during the period July, 1940—May, 1941, does not entirely confirm this impression. An article by Marcel Déat, which appeared in *L'Oeuvre* on November 6, 1940, roughly eight months *before* the German attack on the U.S.S.R., makes the necessary point:

"Our Communists have once again turned nationalist. Their underground leaflets adopt points of view identical to those of the Gaullists. All they are concerned with is the liberation and independence of France, and they hold that only Communism can restore her to full sovereignty. Furthermore, if it is true that the middle and lower middle classes are looking to England, the working classes are turning to Russia and the East for the expected miracles.

"With very much the same grasp of reality, the same critical sense, and an identical hope that everything will be achieved without their having to exert themselves, and above all, without their having to fight."

Add to this what Georges Suarez wrote in *Aujourd'hui* on the following December 31:

"Some people have come to the opinion, not without difficulty and regret, that Gaullism is flourishing and prospering in Communist circles. One had slightly suspected it, but the admission is worth remembering, if only for the unexpected comments that go with it: the Communists would be Anglophiles because of their love of freedom and democracy; they would regard England as the last refuge of traditional beliefs and republican virtues. A likely story. Are we to slip back into the lies and illusions that allowed the Popular Front to emerge and turn itself into an instrument of war against Spain, Germany and Italy? . . .

"Communist love of England does not exist for the reasons that are usually vaunted and declaimed from the rooftops. At the moment, there is no more effective a weapon of disintegration, disorder and disunity in the country than Gaullism. Whoever uses it, knows beforehand he will succeed. The Communists, who are past masters of the art of exploiting mental instability, human degeneration and intellectual confusion, have calculated all the advantages of using Gaullist treason and English propaganda against France."

Now turn to the facts. The struggle against Communist underground activities,[47] which began the day the party was dissolved, was ceaselessly pursued. The bulletin published by police headquarters on November 12, 1940, showed for the period July–October: "543 open arrests, 328 preventive detentions, making a total of 871 arrests; and the uncovering of 35 organizations involving the printing and distribution of leaflets, and seizure of their equipment." The communiqué added:

"A great many former deputies, city councilors, local councilors, suburban councilors and mayors, former secretaries of large federations, heads of sections and cells, important ringleaders, all convicted of underground activities, have been neutralized."

L'OEUVRE,
November 12, 1940

Another communiqué, published eight days later, revealed that during the week of July 1–7 "nine secret organizations for printing and distributing Communist leaflets" had been uncovered. It stated:

"Their members, all active agitators, were arrested and imprisoned in the Santé, and their equipment seized. These operations involved the arrest of 90 activists. Besides which, 63 agitators have been put in preventive detention."

L'OEUVRE,
December 8, 1940

Between July and December 7, 1940, a total of 1141 arrests were made.

A communiqué from police headquarters, published in *Le Matin* on November 29, 1940, reported "a fresh increase in the distribution of underground pamphlets."

A series of watches kept on the Bibliothèque nationale led to the arrest—red-handed—of Gisèle Vallepin, a student, on the twentieth of November. This quickly led to another arrest, that of Jean Commère, a student from the Beaux-Arts.

Announcing this on November 29, *Le Matin* gave

detailed and accurate information on the organization of Communist propaganda in university circles:

"Educational establishments in Paris have been divided into three sections: the head of each section is assisted by an 'expert,' or specialist in this kind of activity.

"The instigator of this dangerous movement was Maurice Delon, an employee at the *mairie* of the third *arrondissement.* His main liaison officers were Jean Rozynaer, a medical student, and Claude Lalet, a student at the Faculté des Lettres.

"The former was in charge of distributing leaflets in all university circles. The latter saw to their compilation and allocation. These backroom agitators had, for these purposes, portable printing machines and considerable stocks of paper.

"The heads of sectors: Bernard Kirschen, Othman Ben Aleya and Claude Lalet—all three students from the Faculté des Lettres—were arrested with their accomplices, all of whom were students of both sexes."

About a month later, the police uncovered a Communist propaganda center in the Paris hospital services. This communiqué, published by *Aujourd'hui* on December 23, 1940, supplied the following details:

"The prime mover of this propaganda group was Jeanne Saloff, a medical student. She gave instructions for the drawing up of leaflets, and organized means of verbal communication with activists working in Public Assistance.

"An employee in the Salpêtrière hospital services, René Leroy, held secret meetings in his house, and also arranged for the distribution of leaflets.

"The treasurership of the organization was in the hands of Élie Hagège, a medical student.

"Louis Rémond, an employee of the hospital services, was responsible for liaison with activists at base.

"Jeanne Saloff, René Leroy, Élie Hagège and Louis Rémond were imprisoned in the Santé.

"Besides this, police headquarters laid hands on another center, which organized underground propaganda in the twentieth *arrondissement.* Ringleaders and others were arrested. Searches led to the seizing of their equipment; in all, sixteen arrests were made."

The intensity of this propaganda worried the editor of *L'Appel*:

"Every morning, carriages in the *métro* are full of mimeographed leaflets.

"Walls of houses are smothered with inscriptions, revolutionary slogans, and hammers and sickles. *L'Humanité* is rearing its head again. Orders from Moscow are passed on by word of mouth in workshops, offices and queues."

July 31, 1941

Equally significant was an article in *Je suis Partout* entitled "Don't Let the Workers Go Communist":

"There is undoubtedly a very great increase in Communist propaganda. It can, of course, be attributed to Moscow's attempts to create incidents with the occupation forces; but, in fact, their propaganda has lately increased with such intensity that some workers must be collaborating with their

Communist leaders in a way they refused to do shortly after the defeat.

"So that even workers who weren't previously Communist are now risking their lives and liberties to help Moscow agents to distribute leaflets and stick up posters. They can also be seen at the gates of metallurgical works in the suburbs aiding and abetting 'lightning meetings' by forming passive groups in front of German sentries or the police, making it impossible for them to arrest the propagandists, who seize the chance of a few minutes' conversation with workers on their way home."

December 6, 1941

La Gerbe echoed this:

"A leaflet headed 'You Must Resist' has been circulating for the last few days. It was first distributed in stations and trains and in the *métro* in the now time-honored way: by several activists and one actual distributor, the others being there to protect their colleague, provided they weren't accused of causing a public disturbance.

"Leaflets are left on seats, thrown into stores, quickly pressed into women's hands, or dropped nonchalantly onto the pavement.

"A passer-by comes along and picks one up. What happens then?

"Up comes a Communist. He tries to make contact, as they say: 'It's true, you know, the Russians are advancing. I know it for a fact that. . . .'

"Another Communist comes up at an agreed point and

joins in. And if the victim's worth it, they try to take it a stage further."

May 28, 1942

Demonstrations, bombs, and bullets

The first shot was fired during the night of August 13 in the Bois de Boulogne. M. Langeron believed it might have been the result of a brawl among the Germans themselves,[48] and there is reason to think he was right.

It was on the following November 11, in the place de l'Étoile, that blood flowed in broad daylight. German soldiers could be seen firing on French students who had formed a procession and were marching toward the Tomb of the Unknown Warrior.

From the very beginning, the Latin Quarter had been hostile to the occupying forces. Young people in the different schools were under pressure simultaneously from both Communist and Gaullist propaganda: their synchronized action was highly effective. *Le France au travail* admitted as much:

"For some weeks, there have been clear signs of a Gaullist attitude on the part of a handful of troublemakers. At first it did not go further than a few outbreaks of rowdyism in classes held by lecturers whose lessons, given in a spirit of European collaboration, displeased a few gangs of agitators. By November 11, the situation had deteriorated."

November 17, 1940

The German authorities had announced that no kind of demonstration would be allowed that day on the public highways. The Vichy government, obeying the conqueror's instructions, ordered all public and private establishments to remain open on November 11 and function normally. On the eighth, the principal of the Académie de Paris passed on this instruction to his subordinates:

"You know that the government has decided that this year, on account of national mourning, work will not cease on the day of November 11. Classes and courses held in the various educational establishments will therefore not cease on that day. There will be no parades. It is agreed that the day should merely be treated as one of solemn meditation. I rely on you to impress on our young people that they must abstain from any kind of demonstration, indoor or outdoor, which might impair not only the solemnity of the commemoration, but the dignity with which they must pursue their studies in our educational establishments."[49]

On the next day, November 9, *La France au travail* wrote:

"At a time when Marshal Pétain is clearly dictating a policy of Franco-German collaboration, murmurs of discontent can be heard in the Latin Quarter, where Jewish-Masonic influences have been at work for some time. We do not question the national sentiments that impel our young students to show their patriotism, but we warn them against any outward demonstration that might play into the hands of Jewish agitators."

These warnings fell on deaf ears.

How many demonstrators were there? *L'Humanité,* on November 11, 1948, gave 50,000 as the figure. The "occupied" press did not go beyond "some hundreds." The truth lies between the two extremes. But where exactly? The only indication, which is vague enough, was given in an account by J. Carcopino, quoting the statement of a German civil servant that there were 150 students among the demonstrators arrested.[50]

The same uncertainty applies to the number of casualties. The English radio, commenting on the incident the following day, put them at eleven dead. *La Résistance des Intellectuels,* a collection published in 1944 by the documentation section of the French Press and Information Service in New York, declared that "a hundred and fifty students were massacred (*sic*) in Paris during the course of a patriotic demonstration on November 11, 1940."[51] J. Carcopino's version differed considerably:

"The Germans, who, on November 11, could have fired their machine guns and strewn the Champs-Élysées with corpses, refrained from committing this crime against an unarmed crowd. They had been given orders to drive back—not massacre—the demonstrators; and when they put their weapons to use, they took care to aim at the lower halves

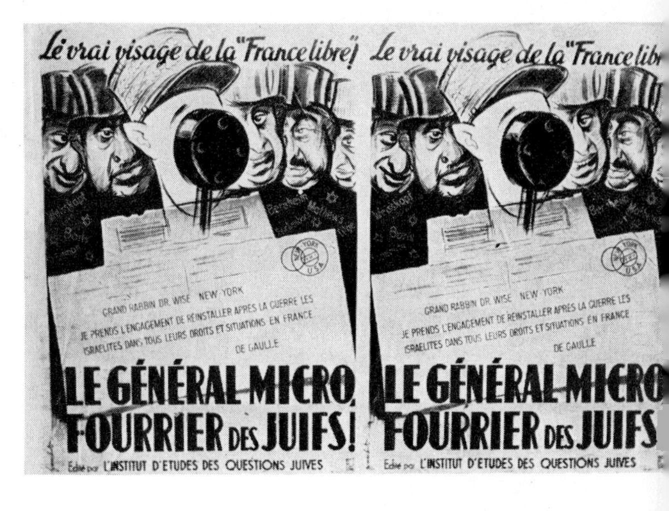

Poster declaiming General De Gaulle and the broadcasts of Free France.

Collaborators greet the legion of anti-Bolshevist volunteers.

Wearing the yellow stars.

Poster at anti-Jewish exhibition, September 1941.

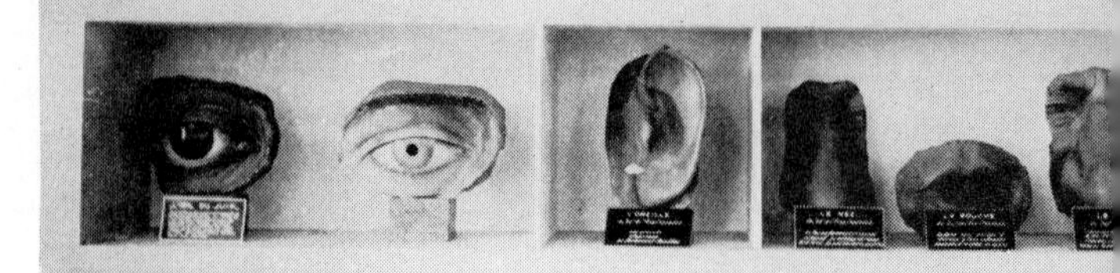

RÉSISTANCE

BULLETIN OFFICIEL DU COMITE NATIONAL DE SALUT PUBLIC

n.1 15 décembre 1940

Résister! C'est le cri qui sort de votre coeur à tous, dans la détresse où vous a laissés le désastre de la Patrie. C'est le cri de vous tous qui ne vous résignez pas, de vous tous qui voulez faire votre devoir.

Mais vous vous sentez isolés et désarmés, et dans le chaos des idées, des opinions et des systèmes, vous cherchez où est votre devoir. Résister, c'est déjà garder son coeur et son cerveau. Mais c'est surtout agir, faire quelque chose qui se traduise en faits positifs, en actes raisonnés et utiles. Beaucoup ont essayé, et souvent se sont découragés en se voyant impuissants. D'autres se sont groupés. Mais souvent leurs groupes se sont trouvés à leur tour isolés et impuissants.

Patiemment, difficilement, nous les avons cherchés et réunis. Ils sont déjà nombreux (plus d'une armée pour Paris seulement), les hommes ardents et résolus qui ont compris que l'organisation de leur effort était nécessaire, et qu'il leur fallait une méthode, une discipline, des chefs.

La méthode? Vous grouper dans vos foyers avec ceux que vous connaissez. Ceux que vous désignerez seront vos chefs. Vos chefs trouveront des hommes éprouvés qui orienteront leurs activités, et qui nous en rendront compte par différents échelons. Notre Comité, pour coordonner vos efforts avec ceux de la France non occupée et ceux qui combattent avec nos Alliés, commandera. Votre tâche immédiate est de vous organiser pour que vous puissiez, au jour où vous en recevrez l'ordre, reprendre le combat. Enrôlez avec discernement les hommes résolus, et encadrez les des meilleurs. Réconfortez et décidez ceux qui doutent ou qui n'osent plus espérer. Recherchez et surveillez ceux qui ont renié la Patrie et qui la trahissent. Chaque jour réunissez et transmettez les informations et les observations utiles pour vos chefs. Pratiquez une discipline inflexible, une prudence constante, une discrétion absolue. Méfiez-vous des inconséquents, des bavards, des traîtres. Ne vous vantez jamais, ne vous confiez pas. Efforcez vous de faire face à vos besoins propres. Nous vous donnerons plus tard des moyens d'action que nous travaillons à rassembler.

En acceptant d'être vos chefs, nous avons fait le serment de tout sacrifier à cette mission, avec dureté, impitoyablement.

Inconnus les uns des autres hier, et dont aucun n'a jamais participé aux querelles des partis d'autrefois aux Assemblées ni aux Gouvernements, indépendants, Français seulement, choisis pour l'action que nous promettons nous n'avons qu'une ambition, qu'une passion, qu'une volonté: faire renaître une France pure et libre.

LE COMITE NATIONAL DE SALUT PUBLIC.

The first Underground newspaper, December 15, 1940.

Pro-De Gaulle inscription, written under movie advertisement, June 1943.

of their legs . . . In 1947, when the Sorbonne remembered all its dead in one holy and solemn commemoration (those who had died in the war and in the Resistance, and those who had been deported), it did not include—and with good reason—any of the supposed victims of November 11, 1940. And when M. Yvon Delbos, in November, 1948, went to the Étoile as Minister of Education, it was not to honor the dead, none of whose names could be cited, but merely to choose a sight for a plaque 'in homage to those pupils, students and teachers who demonstrated against the German invader on November 11, 1940.' "[52]

Must I once again ask where the truth lies? Personally, I see no need. Whether in torrents or drops, blood flowed. That is all that matters. Occupation troops fired on unarmed young Frenchmen. Granted the latter were defying the official orders of the German authorities and knew exactly what they were doing. But although all these boys, steeped in the old Latin Quarter traditions, were ready to stand a few whacks from a baton or rolled cape, as in the past, they certainly never dreamt they would be struck by bullets, even if they were aimed at their feet.

Le Matin, loyally respecting the given warning, printed this account of the incident:

"Elements composed mainly of students made use of November 11 to organize noisy demonstrations in the streets, in spite of the official ban on all demonstrations. This made it necessary for the security forces of the occupation authorities to intervene."

November 16, 1940

La France au travail took a more tolerant attitude:

"These young people let themselves be trapped. . . . We can only hope that the vast majority of our students . . . will be wise enough to keep away from a few dangerous, unthinking, hot-headed kids."

November 17, 1940

Sanctions immediately followed. The Militärbefehlshaber, judging the demonstration incompatible with the dignity of the German army, ordered the closing of all university establishments in Paris. But the Facultés were reopened a month later, and the arrested demonstrators released. The rector, Roussy, was dismissed, and one of the professors, Paul Langevin, was sent to prison because he was thought to have a deplorable influence on French youth.

It has often been asserted that the birth of anti-German terrorism in Paris was the direct and immediate result of the Soviet Union's entry into the war. Dates seem to support this assertion: the first terrorist act in Paris was on August 13, 1941—that is, two months after the opening of the Russian campaign. But it must be noted that the first Communist to be shot was led to the firing squad on July 19, and the second on the twenty-fourth—in other words, after the fateful date of the twenty-second of June. Must it therefore be assumed that the Germans waited until their armies had attacked the Russians before shooting French Communists? In any case, they were the ones who shot first.

The starting date of this relentless struggle, which went on for three successive years in a veritable maze of Paris streets, can be pinpointed as July 14, 1941. On that day, a peaceful, though covertly aggressive, demonstration took place near the place de la République. Many of the marchers were wearing tricolor badges and someone even sang the *Marseillaise.* The German authorities judged this undesirable, and set about making a number of arrests. In order to persuade its readers that the demonstration was really inspired by foreign elements, *Le Franciste* under the heading, "A Fine Batch of Patriots," gave the names and nationalities of the demonstrators arrested "for flaunting the French national colors." Among them were six Polish Jews, five Armenians, four Spaniards, three Italians and a Turk. Not one Frenchman. But ten days later, André Masseron, a French worker, was shot for singing the *Marseillaise* on the same occasion.

The first combat groups in Paris were built up during the second half of July, 1941—by order of the Komintern, it has often been said, referring to Stalin's famous order of the day which prescribed the setting up in every Russian locality occupied by the Germans of partisan forces designed to fight the enemy by every available means. This order, which was spread by the underground radio, could not have remained unknown. But even allowing that the Communist party leaders would have applied it to the letter in French occupied territory, it must be said it was not implemented, at the outset, by very many skilled practitioners. André Ouzoulias, who was one of the first initiators of these combat groups, admitted, shortly after the liberation:

> "At that time (that is to say, July–August, 1941), few understood the need for replying to the enemy other than by words or through apathy. At the beginning, there were twenty or thirty fighting with arms in Paris."[53]

The originator of these terrorist groups was a boy of sixteen, Gilbert Brulstein, a member of the Young Communists. The indictment brought against the seven terrorists accused on March 4, 1942 (which will be discussed later on) pointed out that Brulstein had conceived the idea of creating a force of voluntary gunmen: mobile groups of about three hundred men. He taught his recruits how to handle and strip down a revolver, and how to read a map. A search of his room revealed 150 revolvers, 25 kilos of dynamite and 10 infernal machines (See *Les Nouveaux Temps,* March 5 and 6, 1942).

His program had three objectives: (1) Attempts on the lives of German army personnel. (2) Execution of traitors and renegades. (3) Sabotage of factories and railroads. In the early days of August, he was joined by a colleague of note. Pierre Georges (or Fabien), aged 22, a veteran of the Spanish Civil War, who had escaped from the camp at Baillet, where he had been interned, and who had come to

Paris and had gotten in touch with Brulstein. Together they organized the attack on the Barbès *métro* station, which cost the life of a German soldier. Fabien was in charge of the execution, Brulstein of the planning. The operation was a complete success, and the assailants got away safely.[54]

Executions of renegades began in early September. Marcel Gitton was the first to go. He had been a member of the Communist party Central Committee since 1928, and three years later was elected to the Secretariat. He broke with his comrades when they were persecuted in November, 1939, got in touch with the Germans at the beginning of the occupation, and founded a short-lived Workers and Peasants' party. Fernand Soupé, mayor of Montreuil, also a member of the Communist party Central Committee, and later a confirmed Doriotist, was the next to be struck down, but survived a serious wound. By contrast, Albert Clément, formerly of *L'Humanité* and the *Cri du peuple,* where he had surpassed himself as a Jew-baiter and a Communist-baiter, was shot down in the very heart of Paris on a spring afternoon, and never rose again.

Simultaneously with Brulstein's organization, another, composed entirely of Jewish Communists, went into action. It was led by a boy of seventeen, Marcel Rayman, whose short, meteoric life is inadequately known. He was responsible for the most important terrorist action in occupied Europe (excluding the assassination of Heydrich, "the Police Chief," in Prague): on July 28, 1942, aided by a

Spaniard, Celestino, and an Italian, Fontano, he hurled a bomb into the car of Schaumburg, the general commanding Greater Paris, killing him on the spot. Two months later, seconded by the same two comrades, Rayman struck at President Ritter, Gauleiter Sauckel's representative in France who was responsible for sending forced labor to Germany. After pursuing his task of assassination for over a year, he was arrested at the end of 1943 and shot.[55] A company of F.T.P.'s was named after him at the liberation.

Coördination of combat groups made up of foreign immigrants was in the hands of Misaak Manouchian, an Armenian. He was a man of thirty-five, serious-minded, methodical, endowed with steely courage and ferocious energy. He was greatly respected by members of the organization. The Germans called him "the head of the foreign gang," as he was styled by the famous poster that appeared on the walls of Paris after his trial, and credited him with sixty attacks, resulting in 150 dead and 600 wounded. This terrorist was a lover of poetry and himself wrote verse. In a letter that he sent to his wife before going to his execution, he made only one request: that his friends would one day publish his poems. This wish has never been fulfilled.

Following the attack on the Barbès *métro* station, the occupied press was given orders to stir up public opinion and direct it against the Moscow-inspired killers. This was what *La Gerbe* said, on August 28, 1941:

"There has been an assassination. Hostages have been seized. The nightmare is beginning. Paris has remained calm for a year; it was the whole country that mattered. That concerned only the French, not the Communists.

"But now that both have been hunted down, they have taken action. For them, taking action means killing. Their aim is to bring down reprisals, agony and terror on Paris; they want to make sure they won't be the only ones to perish in our ruins.

"Arrest them now! The choice must be made. Not tomorrow, but this minute. Permit treason and apathy, and within an hour, possibly, our fellow countrymen will be arrested at random and sent to prison. Therefore, act! Take sides energetically against this crime. Help those who are mercilessly tracking them down. You will be defending your city, your homes and your lives. They may cause the shedding of our blood: they must not therefore be shot like soldiers, with German bullets, but die like the traitors they are, at the hands of a French firing squad."

To drive home the point, *La Gerbe* also hired a journalist to explain to their readers how these killers operated. After a close investigation, this is what he discovered:

"When a series of 'combat groups' gets the order to liquidate someone, its headquarters makes a study of how the intended victim spends his time.

"Information about his habits and movements is collected. Apparently trivial conversations with his concierge, or the people he shops from, visits on vague pretexts (house-to-house canvassing, charity calls, sales of various objects, black market propositions, and so on), calling him by phone and then hanging up—any means of organizing a system of checks and cross-checks is used. In this way, the victim's timetable and itinerary is compiled. This is completed and verified by having him shadowed.

"The chosen killer is usually kept out of these preparatory stages. It is obviously undesirable that he should be seen or observed in places where he would later be operating or noticed by his victim. On the other hand, he has to know exactly what his man looks like so as to be able to act swiftly, as during the course of a brief meeting, or in bad visibility, as at dusk.

"Either someone is chosen who knows the person in question . . . or the killer is posted with 'witnesses' who point the victim out as he passes by. This is further completed by the use of photos. In this way, the killer learns the victim's various clothes, different hair styles, and so on. . . . These meticulous preparations insure that the operation will be rapidly and effectively carried out.

"Knowing the victim's timetable means that members of the combat group can take up their positions well in advance. In every case, arrangements are made to forestall pursuit. The killer, depending on the circumstances, is either posted at a spot where the victim will appear, or on his route, or sometimes close by; in this last case, an accomplice gives him the signal when and where to strike.

"Once this is done, the killer makes off as fast as possible by the best escape route, which depends on where he fired from, and from which direction people hearing the shot are likely to come. If necessary, he is shielded by accomplices. Then they all disperse rapidly. In the event that the area is cordoned off too quickly for the killer to make his escape, a number of hiding places can be arranged close by."

LA GERBE,
June 11, 1942

From September, 1941, onward, these attacks were stepped up. The Germans replied by executing hostages, which in turn led to fresh waves of terrorism. It became a vicious circle from which neither side would disengage. The ratio of victims to hostages shot was hopelessly disproportionate, but the Communists did not care. Colonel Rémy asked one of the F.T.P. leaders, "Do you think it pays to have five or ten of your people shot for the sake of capturing a revolver or a rifle?" and was told, "Yes, because every time we announce that five or ten of our people have been shot, the F.T.P. enrolls fifty to a hundred new members."[56]

In order to impress public opinion still further, the German authorities organized a series of terrorist trials with all the trappings of "judicial procedure": the prisoners were given lawyers (chosen, of course, from the personnel of the Verwaltungstab in the Hôtel Majestic), and journalists were invited to attend sessions of the tribunal.

The first trial opened on March 4, 1942, and lasted two days. It involved seven members of the Brulstein organization; Roger Hanlet, Robert Peltier, Tony Bloncourt, Pierre Milan, Acher Somahya and Fernand Zalkinow let themselves be captured so their leader could escape the clutches of the German police. *Les Nouveaux Temps* gave a detailed account of the trial. This account was obviously inspired by the indictment that was read at the first hearing and that began as follows:

"The accused, all French nationals, are seven in number, including one Jew, and one half-Jew. All belong to the Communist party. They have perpetrated every kind of attack on the German army, and it has been established from the accusation files that, in the actions of which they were guilty, they were inspired not by patriotic motives, but by slavish obedience to article 25 of the Communist party program drawn up at the Sixth Congress in Moscow in 1928 . . . These are not, therefore, ordinary terrorists, but assailants belonging to a group which was fully organized even before the German occupation and authorized to commit misdeeds and crimes under any government, provided it was in accordance with the dictates of the Kremlin."

March 5, 1942

Naturally, they were all condemned to death. The court's findings specifically mentioned:

"It was not a question of serving France, but of serving Bolshevism. Sentence is not, therefore, passed on French patriots, but on social criminals."

LE CRI DU PEUPLE,
March 6, 1942

Albert Clément, who took it on himself to report the trial in his *Cri du peuple*, noticed that when the public had withdrawn just before the verdict was given, "the accused showed a disconcertingly cynical attitude by laughing and joking." Three months later, he was himself to be killed.

The second trial was held on April 14. There were twenty-seven prisoners: Marcel Bertone, Gilbert Bourdarias, Louis Coquillet, Pierre Touati, Pierre Tourette, René Toyer, Louis Marchandise, Spartaco Guisco, Pierre Tirot, Yves Kermen, Ricardo Robregger, Mario Buzzi, Simone Schloss, Alfred Congnon, Léon Landsaght, Emile Lefebvre, Marie Lefebvre, Pierre Leblois, Georges Tondelier, Karl Schoenaar, Jean Quarre, Camille Drouvot, Raymond Tardif, André Aubouet, Jean Garreau, Laurant (Christian name unknown) and André Kirschen.

These "audience impressions" appeared in *La Gerbe*:

"None of these terrorists, with their criminal faces and bloodstained hands, denied what they had done—except Jean Garreau, the one whose guilt was most conclusively established. But they suddenly became evasive when questioned as to who supplied them with orders and money.

" 'Funds?'

" 'Pierre gave them to me to pass on to Jacques.'

"The same with everything else. Names and nicknames in the organization are constantly being changed, and it is difficult to follow a thread that keeps snapping.

"The business of the explosives, too, is like a game of hunt-the-slipper. . . . It passes through half a dozen hands, and ends up with Loulou—that's all that's known about her—and she passes the stuff on to her friend Simone, who hurries off to give it to Marie. But this time the homicidal paper chase leads somewhere—to Simone and Marie. These two women, Schloss and Lefebvre, are activists; the former has already been sentenced for distributing leaflets. The bomb affair will send her straight to the firing squad."

April 23, 1942

She did go there, with twenty-four of her friends.

After reading the sentence, the president of the tribunal thanked the lawyers, "whose task has been so difficult," and made the following little speech:

"The accused have organized and undertaken the making of bombs and storing of arms. It has been proved during the course of the trial that they belonged to the Communist party, and even to a special organization at the party's very core. In this special organization they have assumed military tasks; they regard themselves as soldiers for Communism, and, as such, have learnt weapon training, and have been instructed in methods of attack, throwing bombs, ground reconnaissance, map reading, and so on. . . .

"They have been guilty of attacks, arson, cutting military cables, attempts to murder not only members of the German army, but Frenchmen as well. Their combat methods have been particularly cowardly. Not only had they no intention of helping the French people by their crimes, but they had no regard whatsoever for their own countrymen.

"All those who know Communism realize that every party member is a traitor to his own country. The accused cannot argue that they have been misled, because each one had in him a propensity to crime, and hoped to satisfy his baser instincts in the Communist party fold."

LE CRI DU PEUPLE,
April 15, 1942

The occupation authorities did not consider the proceedings sufficiently effective, so the idea was later abandoned, and hostages were again tried and shot as civilians. This meant that young Christians, who knew nothing of bombs or assassinations, were sent to the firing squad with the utmost discretion, and never benefited from the vast publicity lavished on the Jews and Communists.

Epilogue

The Paris press—at least, that part of it which was read openly—reported, in typical fashion, the story of the Resistance movement, the trials (the trial of the "twenty-three" in February, 1944), and sanctions taken by the Germans (the "twenty-three" were shot on the twenty-first of February). Some pages were devoted exclusively to the terrorists (see p. 2: *Le Matin* for April 17, 1944), while the rest of the paper contained propaganda articles, official decrees, and information about rationing.

Attacks and reprisals multiplied. While the "occupied" press, posters and the German radio qualified and distorted news of collapsing fronts and invaded areas, the core of the Resistance was organized and developed in conjunction with other parts of the country and the Allies. German propaganda had to contend with news broadcasts by the B.B.C. and the Free French Radio that contradicted their own reports. The underground press passed on information to partisans in the interior and to the Parisians themselves about the heroism of unknown freedom fighters in their native towns, or about the progress of the liberation forces in Normandy, or in the south or east. German threats, trials, announcements and reprisals disgusted some and inspired others to further efforts. Forty-two young people were shot on August 16, 1944, in the Bois de Boulogne; but their friends intensified the struggle when the Germans began to evacuate Paris amid strikes and uprisings. The Paris uprising began on the nineteenth; Leclerc's tanks were approaching. The occupation papers stopped appearing on the nineteenth, and were replaced on August 21 by the Resistance press.

APPENDIX

CHRONOLOGY

1940

June 14	German troops enter Paris.
June 15	The Pigalle movie house reopens.
June 17	Birth of the "occupied" press: the new *Matin* begins publication.
June 18	Hitler visits Paris.
June 19	The Germans search the apartments of Edouard Daladier, Georges Mandel and Paul Reynaud.
June 20	Cars are requisitioned by the German authorities.
June 21	Parisians hear the armistice announcement.

June 23 Hitler's second visit to Paris.

June 24 Classes begin again at the Conservatoire. The Bibliothèque nationale reopens.

June 26 The Germans demolish the statue of General Mangin.

July 4 William Bullitt, the American ambassador, leaves Paris for Vichy.

July 6 The Casino de Paris reopens.

July 7 The Seine préfecture takes a census of the Paris population.

July 11 The Théâtre de l'Oeuvre reopens; revival of J. Bassan's *Juliette.*

July 12 The Concert Mayol reopens.

July 13 Offices of the Grand Orient are searched.

July 14 First anniversary, during the occupation, of the capture of the Bastille is silently observed.

July 16 Banks function normally again.

July 20 All chief representatives of the German military and civil authorities gather at the Palais-Bourbon to hear Hitler's speech to the Reichstag.

July 22 Dr. Goebbels visits Paris.

July 26 The Théâtre des Ambassadeurs reopens; revival of M. Duran's *Nous ne sommes pas mariés* (see pp. 61-62).

July 31 The Théâtre de la Madeleine reopens; revival of Sacha Guitry's *Pasteur* (see p. 124).

August 22 The Opéra Comique reopens; *Carmen* is performed.

August 23 General de la Laurencie, appointed delegate general of the Vichy government to occupied territory, arrives in Paris.

August 24 The Opéra reopens; *The Damnation of Faust* is performed.

September 7	The Comédie Française reopens; discussion and poetry reading is held.
September 25	A coöperative for the Paris daily press set up.
October 6	Cardinal Suhard enthroned.
October 12	Racing begins again.
November 1	General Otto von Stülpnagel is made Commander-in-Chief, Occupied Zone.
November 11	Student demonstration in the place de l'Étoile (see pp. 160-164).
November 12	The Facultés closed.
November 13	Professor Paul Langevin is arrested (see p. 164).
November 21	Revival of the Folies-Bergère grand revue.
November 29	The Reichsleiter, Alfred Rosenberg, speaks to the French section of the National Socialist Orangization from the platform of the Palais-Bourbon.
December 15	The National Committee of Public Safety secretly prints the first issue of its newspaper, *Résistance.* Concert by the Radio-Stuttgart Orchestra at the Palais de Chaillot. L'Aiglon's ashes arrive in Paris.
December 18	General de la Laurencie hands over the command of his delegation to F. de Brinon.
December 20	The Académie Française awards prizes for virtue, and recompenses large families.
December 22	The Monet-Rodin Exhibition opens at the Orangerie.
December 23	First execution: Jacques Bonsergent, engineer, is shot "for an act of violence against a member of the German army." The occupation authorities allow restaurants and cafés to stay open till 2:30 A.M. on Christmas Eve. Traffic to cease at 3:00 A.M.

December 29	"Marshal's Day": pictures of Marshal Pétain on sale in Paris streets in aid of National Relief.

1941

January 4	Bergson dies at his Paris home.
March 21	Gala of the Union des Artistes at Bagatelle.
May 1	The Germans celebrate Labor Day at the Palais de Chaillot.
May 10	André Antoine Gala at the Comédie Française.
May 11	Jewish Institute of Studies opens.
May 18	The Berlin Staatsoper presents Mozart's *Abduction from the Seraglio* at the Opéra.
May 23	Parisians informed that in the future restaurants are to be divided into four categories.
July 1	Windows of the German bookstore "Rive-Gauche" are smashed.
July 8	Déat, Doriot and other "heads" decide to form a Legion of French Volunteers to fight on the Russian front.
July 14	Demonstration in the place de la République area; arrests are made.
July 19	Roig, a mechanic, is shot for insults to the German army.
July 24	André Masseron, a worker, is shot for singing the *Marseillaise* on the fourteenth of July.
August 13	Demonstration at the porte St. Denis. A German officer is killed near the porte d'Orléans.

August 19	Two young Communists, Henri Gautherot and Samuel Tyszelman, who were arrested after the demonstration of August 13, are shot.
August 20	Raid on the eleventh *arrondissement:* 4,300 Jews, including 1,300 French Jews, are sent to Drancy.
August 21	A German officer is murdered on the platform of the Barbès *métro* station.
August 23	The Vichy government sets up special courts for trying Communists.
August 27	The Paris Court sentences three Communists to death.
August 29	Count d'Estienne d'Orves, sent from London by the Free French Navy, is arrested and shot with two of his colleagues: Barbier, a businessman, and Doornik, a Dutchman.
August 30	Five Communists are shot for taking part in the demonstration of August 13.
September 3	A German officer is murdered.
September 4	Marcel Gitton, former secretary of the Communist party working for the Germans, is shot dead.
September 6	A German officer is murdered. Three hostages are shot.
September 10	Attack on a member of the German army.
September 11	Attack on a member of the German army.
September 16	A German officer is murdered. Ten hostages are shot.
September 20	Twelve hostages are shot, including a lawyer, Georges Pitard, who was legal adviser to the Seine Trade Union Movement.
September 24	Jean Catelas, member of the Communist party Central Committee, is guillotined in the prison courtyard of the Santé.

November 21	Bomb explosion in the German bookstore "Rive-Gauche."
December 15	Gabriel Péri is shot. Jacques Grunbaum, a lawyer, is shot.
December 20	Académie Goncourt election: Pierre Champion is elected by six votes to three against André Billy.
December 22	Fernand Soupé, former member of the Communist party Central Committee, later a Doriotist, is wounded by a revolver shot.

1942

January 7	A bomb is thrown at German army installations.
January 8	A policeman is shot in the Boulevard Magenta.
January 9	A bomb is thrown at German army installations.
January 16	A bomb is thrown at German army installations.
January 18	A German soldier is wounded by revolver shots.
January 20	A German soldier is wounded by revolver shots.
January 23	Boris Vildé and Anatole Levitsky, ethnologists at the Musée de l'Homme and founders of the National Committee of Public Safety, are shot. Five hostages are shot, including a lawyer, Léon Nordmann.
January 28	A bomb attack on German army installations.

January 29 — An official order of General Schaumburg announces the deportation to the east of "a hundred members of the Jewish Communist Youth," and the shooting of "six Communists and Jews."

February 20 — *Le Silence de la Mer* is published secretly.

February 28 — General Otto von Stülpnagel relieved of his command and replaced by his cousin, General Heinrich von Stülpnagel, former president of the Wiesbaden Armistice Commission.

March 1 — A German soldier is murdered.

March 3 — Paris suburbs are raided by the Royal Air Force.

March 4 — Burial of the German soldier murdered on the first of March. On the occasion, General Schaumburg publishes an official order declaring: "In reprisal for this treacherous murder, twenty Communists and Jews, from the same section of society as the assailants, will be shot. Twenty more will be put to death if the murderers are not discovered before March 16, 1942." Trial of seven terrorists from Brulstein's group opens (see p. 171).

March 8 — Funeral services are held for victims of the air raid of the third of March.

March 9 — Fernand Zalkinov, eighteen, a student at the École Arago and an active Communist, is shot.

March 10 — Demonstration at the Lycée Buffon. Five pupils are arrested: Arthus, Baudry, Benoît, Grelot and Legros.

April 2 — A German sentry is murdered, and a bomb is thrown into a building occupied by German troops. Five Communists are immediately shot "by way of reprisal."

April 4 — The Franco-German Exhibition, "La Vie Nouvelle," opens at the Grand Palais.

April 8 — A German officer is murdered.

April 12 — General Schaumburg announces: "If the author (of the attack on April 2), has not been arrested by April 17, 1942, a number of collectively responsible persons, Jews and Communists, will be shot."

April 14 — Trial of the "Twenty-Seven" (see p. 173).

April 20 — A German officer murdered at the Molitor *métro* station.

April 21 — General Schaumburg announces: "As a result (of this murder), I order the following: (a) Ten Communists and Jews, or persons collectively responsible, will be shot immediately. (b) If, eight days after the publication of this notice, the culprit has not been arrested, twenty Communists and Jews, collectively responsible, will be put to death. (c) Five hundred Communists, Jews or persons collectively responsible will be deported to the east to forced labor camps. (d) All places of entertainment, theaters and movie houses will be closed from today until 5 A.M. on Friday, the twenty-fourth of April."

April 22 — Further official order from General Schaumburg: "French civilians have arrested and handed over to the police the culprits of April 20, 1942. The population has shown in this case that it was willing to coöperate in the apprehension of the murderers, thus avoiding reprisal measures. As a result, I order the following: (1) The twenty Communists and Jews collectively responsible for the attack of April 20, 1942, will not be shot. (2) The measures affecting the closing of all places of entertainment, theaters and movie houses until Friday, April 24, are lifted forthwith."

May 18 Death of Cardinal Baudrillart.

May 30 Jacques Decour, Georges Politzer, and Jacques Solomon are shot.

May 31 The "Women's Revolt" in the rue de Buci.

June 1 Order by the Militärbefehlshaber forbidding all Jews over the age of six to appear in public without a yellow star.

June 2 Albert Clément, the Doriotist, is killed.

June 7 Order relative to the wearing of yellow stars becomes effective.

June 10 The State Tribunal passes sentence in the rue de Buci affair: five death sentences (one in the prisoner's absence), six sentenced to hard labor for life, two to twenty years' hard labor, one to ten years, three to five years and three acquittals. The Bouffes-Parisiennes announce the one hundred and ninetieth performance of *Une jeune fille savait,* and the Châtelet the four hundredth performance of *Valses de Vienne.*

June 11 Marcel Déat's conference at the "Bolshevism versus Europe" exhibition, is arranged at the Salle Wagram by the Committee for Anti-Bolshevik Action.

June 18 Raid on Menilmontant: ninety Communists are arrested.

June 22 Laval speaks to Paris workers: "France cannot remain passive and indifferent to the huge sacrifices Germany is making to create a Europe in which we have a vital part to play."

July 10 General Oberg, recently appointed "Hoehere S.S. und Polizeiführer im Bereich des Militärbefehlshaber in Frankreich," introduces himself as follows: "I am determined to guarantee the French people, without reserve, and under conditions of total war, continuity of work in peace and safety. But I have ascertained that it is the close friends and relatives of assailants, saboteurs and troublemakers, who have been helping them both before and after their crimes. I have therefore decided to inflict the severest penalties not only on the assailants, saboteurs and troublemakers themselves, but in the event of their escaping and as soon as their names are known, on the families of these criminals should they fail to report to a German or French police station within ten days of the crime. I therefore announce the following penalties: (1) All close male relatives in ascending line, including brothers-in-law and cousins over the age of eighteen, will be shot. (2) All similarly related females will be sentenced to hard labor. (3) All children of men and women affected by these measures, who are under the age of seventeen, will be put in reform schools."

July 16 The huge Jewish rally at the Vélodrome de Paris (see p. 148). Reopening of the Florence, a night club, provides "one of the most striking events of the last two weeks in the world of entertainment."

July 28 A bomb, thrown by Marcel Rayman, a

	young Jew, kills General Schaumburg (see p. 168).
July 29	Roger Pironneau, a student at the Catholic Institute who was arrested on August 17, 1941, and sentenced to death "for spying and intelligence activities with the enemy," is shot.
August 1	Peters-Matisse, a twenty-two-year-old painter, is shot.
August 9	Dr. Bursztyn, leader of the Association of Jewish Intellectuals and Students, and Nadler, a journalist who is editor of *Notre Voix,* a Jewish underground newspaper, are shot.
August 11	General Oberg addresses Parisians: "In spite of constant warnings, the peace has once again been disturbed. . . . Consequently, ninety-three terrorists who were convicted of acts of terrorism, or of being accessories, have been shot on my orders. I ask the French population, in their own interests, to exert the utmost vigilance in the uncovering of terrorist plots. Failing this, I shall be forced to take measures affecting the entire population."
August 19	*Fête des Caf'Conc'* in the Parc des Princes.
August 22	André Diez, twenty-one-year-old assistant chemist and leader of the Latin Quarter F.T.P., is shot.
September 19	Champion, member of the F.T.P., is shot.
October 21	Jean Lefèvre and Paul Thierret, F.T.P. members, are shot.

1943

January 5	Electricity is rationed.
January 11	Thirty *métro* stations are closed.
January 16	The Committee for the Organization of Entertainments decrees that all places of entertainment (except national theaters) shall be closed one day a week.
January 17	The rue Henri Heine (sixteenth *arrondissement*) becomes the rue Jean-Sébastien Bach.
January 18	Exhibtion of "Lotteries, Past and Present" opens at the Orangerie.
January 30	Germans in Paris meet at the Palais de Chaillot to celebrate the tenth anniversary of the Third Reich.
February 8	Arthus, Baudry, Benoît, Grelot, pupils of the Lycée Buffon, and Legros, pupil of the École Alsacienne, arrested the previous tenth of March (see entry for March 10, 1942), are shot.
February 9	Sale of "cooked meals" and imposition of the "metal tax."
February 13	Two German officers are murdered.
February 14	All places of entertainment "known as cabarets" are closed for a week as a reprisal.
February 15	Communists Gannat, Hamel, Le Ballanger, Vacher, Van der Heyden are shot. Enforced registration in Paris of Frenchmen born between January 1, 1912, and December 31, 1921.

February 27 — *La Nuit de Cinéma* at the Gaumont-Palace.

March 1 — The "National Revolutionary Front" decides to create a militia to reply to the "Communist peril" with the use of force.

March 31 — Sale of radios is forbidden.

April 4 — Air raid on the Paris suburbs.

April 15 — At the Hôtel Drouot, the cap that Louis XVI wore at the Temple is sold for 12,500 francs, and one of Marie Antoinette's necklaces, for 140,000 francs.

May 10 — Handgrenade attack in front of the Odéon.

May 27 — First meeting of the National Resistance Committee (at No. 48 rue du Four).

June 2 — A German colonel is killed in broad daylight near the Madeleine.

June 18 — At the Hôtel Drouot, a painting "in the style of Velasquez," is auctioned off for 300,000 francs, and a small Louis XV cupboard for 240,000 francs.

June 30 — Exhibition of period posters opens at the Musée Galliera.

July 14 — Air raid on the Paris suburbs.

August 8 — Doriotists parade in the Champs-Élysées. Their "leader" gives his order of the day: "More than a hundred thousand Parisians, from the Étoile to the rue des Pyramides, have saluted our glorious flags. Men of the French Guards, men and women party activists, I am proud of you."

August 16 — Air raid on the Paris suburbs.

September 3 — Air raid on Paris.

September 9 — A grenade is thrown into the Doriotist headquarters in the rue Lamarck; fifteen are wounded.

September 29 — President Ritter is killed (see p. 168).

October 6 — The following are shot: Henri Bajsztok,

	Communist F.T.P.; André Chassagne, Communist F.T.P.; Marcel Dutet, leader of an F.T.P. group; Georges Gauthier, Christian F.T.P.; Alexandre Honvault, Communist F.T.P.; Pierre Lamandé, an agricultural expert, one of the heads of the F.T.P.; Jean Poiré, Communist F.T.P.; Maurice Priolley, Communist F.T.P.; Louis Wallé, regional commander of the F.T.P.; and Claude Warocquier, Christian J.O.C.
October 23	The following are shot: George Bauce, nineteen, leader of a combat group; Alfred Dequéant, twenty-five, denounced for distributing leaflets and receiving arms; and Roger Poncelet, twenty-three, leader of an F.T.P. group.
October 27	Bomb attack on a German military convoy.
October 30	Count Robert de Voguë is arrested "for intelligence activity with terrorists groups."
December 1	The Occupied Paris society gathers at the Comédie Française for the dress rehearsal of Claudel's *Soulier de Satin.*
December 31	Air raid.

1944

January 31	Death of Jean Giraudoux.
February 14	Paul Faure, F.T.P. captain, is shot.
February 17	First day of the trial of "the twenty-three foreign terrorists": Alfonso Celestino (former soldier in the Spanish Republican

army), Golda Bancic (woman philosophy student), Della Negra (Italian-born, naturalized Frenchman), Thomas Elek (Hungarian, "in charge of train derailments"), Fingerwaïg (Polish immigrant), Spartaco Fontano (Italian), Glasz (Hungarian), Léon Goldberg (Polish), Grzywacz (Polish), Kubazki (Polish), Luccarini (Italian), Manukian (Armenian), Misaak Manouchian (Armenian-born, naturalized Frenchman, the most important prisoner; see p. 168), Martinniak (Polish), Marcel Rayman (head of the Jewish Communist combat group; see p. 167), Boczow (Hungarian), Salvadori (Italian), Szapiro (Polish), Usseglio (Italian), Waisbrot (Polish), Robert Witchitz (Polish-born, naturalized Frenchman). Two Frenchmen, Georges Cloarec and Roger Rouxel, were associated with them.

The accused, whose ages ranged from 18 to 25, were mostly workers. Each of them is given a short biographical note in *Pages de gloire des vingt-trois,* published by the French Committee for the Protection of Immigrants.

February 21 The accused twenty-three are shot. Golda Bancic was not executed, but deported to Germany, where she was later decapitated with an ax.

March 5 Max Jacob, the poet, dies at Drancy.

March 7 Georges Citerne, an actor (known as Georges Eric) in command of an F.T.P. group, is shot. Fifteen more members of the F.T.P. are shot on the same day.

March 15	Thirty-two F.T.P. members are sentenced to death. (One of them is not to be executed because of his age: sixteen.)
March 17	One of the condemned, Michel François, is shot.
March 23	Another of the condemned, René Roechel (or Rajac), is shot.
March 24	Twenty more condemned F.T.P. members are shot, including Paul Quillet, F.T.P. regional commander.
April 11	Three F.T.P. members are shot: Jean Alezard, A. Dreyer and Jean François (aged seventeen).
April 20	Air raid.
April 21	Emmanuel Bourneuf, a fifty-year-old workman, is shot.
April 25	Louis Chapiro, F.T.P. commander, and Jean Camus, aged eighteen and a Christian F.T.P. member, are shot.
April 26	Marshal Pétain comes to Paris to attend the funeral services for the victims of the air raid of April 20.
May 20	Jean Fournier, F.T.P. member, is shot.
June 2	Jean Bosc, aged eighteen, a section leader in the F.T.P. company "Alsace-Lorraine," and Jean Calvet, nineteen, group leader in the same company, are shot.
June 28	Philippe Henriot is murdered.
July 1	Two F.T.P. members, Georges Hercwyn and Eugène Janneton, are shot.
July 15	Mutiny in the Santé, in the "common law" block.
August 8	Laval comes to Paris to arrange a meeting of the National Assembly.
August 9	The Germans begin to evacuate Paris.
August 10	Strike by Paris railway workers.

August 12	Charity ball at the Palais-Royal in aid of needy artists.
August 15	Strike by the Paris police.
August 16	Forty-two young people, including nine students (among them three J.E.C. members: Jean Desgorges, Jean Dudraisil and Jean Gay) are shot at the Cascade in the Bois de Boulogne.
August 17	Laval leaves Paris under German escort.
August 18	The occupation papers suspend publication.
August 19	First day of the Paris uprising.
August 21	Resistance papers on sale.
August 25	General Leclerc's tanks enter Paris. The German general in command surrenders at 2:45 P.M.

NAMES AND CIRCULATION OF PARIS NEWSPAPERS

The *Annuaire de la Presse* for the years 1942–1943 listed six hundred periodicals appearing in Paris during that period. They were classified as follows:

Political dailies	9
Weeklies, and political and literary reviews	16
Administrative papers and others (legal and judicial announcements, public finance, local government, public works, pensions and son on)	61

Academic publications	41
Agriculture	37
Architecture	7
Army	2
Bibliography	5
Charity	6
Colonies	3
Crafts	9
Educational and domestic	15
Electricity and radio	45
Fashions	13
Finance	13
Fine Arts, interior decoration and furniture	6
Friendly societies	12
Games, hobbies and children's papers	7
Illustrated and family magazines	11
Industry and economic questions	59
Insurance	8
Jurisprudence	34
Medicine and natural sciences	77
Navy, navigation and fishing	7
Paper manufacture	2
Pharmacy	6
Philately	1
Photography	3
Religion	3
Sport	40
Tourism and transport	7
Theater, music and the movies	8
Trade	88
Foreign language newspapers	6
Various reviews and weeklies	15

Only those publications are mentioned here that either were founded under the occupation, or made a "fresh start," and attracted, under various names, the interest of Parisian readers.

L'Appel. Weekly, 1941–1944.
Aujourd'hui. Daily, 1940–1944.
Au Pilori. Weekly, 1940–1944.
Comœdia. Weekly, reappeared on June 21, 1941.
Le Cri du peuple. Daily, 1940–1944.
Les Dernières Nouvelles de Paris. Daily, first appeared on June 20, 1940; ceased publication on the following sixteenth of September.
Le Fait. Weekly, 1940–1944.
La France au travail. Daily, 1940–1944; changed its title on November 10, 1941, and became *La France socialiste.*
France-Europe, "Organ of French unity through national revolution." Weekly, 1942–1944.
La France socialiste. See *La France au travail.*
Le Franciste. Weekly, 1941–1944.
La Gerbe. Weekly, 1940–1944.
Germinal. Weekly, April–August 1944.
L'Illustration. Weekly, reappeared in Paris on August 10, 1940.
Je suis Partout. Weekly, reappeared on February 7, 1941.
La Jeunesse. Weekly, 1941–1944.
Le Matin. Daily, reappeared on June 17, 1940.
Les Nouveaux Temps. Daily, 1940–1944.
L'Oeuvre. Daily, reappeared in Paris on September 21, 1940.
Paris-Midi. Daily, reappeared on February 17, 1941.
Paris-Soir. Daily, 1940–1944.
Pariser-zeitung. Daily, published in German with some pages in French.
Le Petit Parisien. Daily, reappeared on October 8, 1940.
Le Réveil du peuple. Bi-monthly, 1940–1942.
La Révolution nationale. Daily, 1941–1944.
La Tempête, organ of *Le Feu,* "working for *Les Hommes*

du Feu in order to prepare the *Temps du Feu.*" Daily, published its first number (a free issue) on January 21, 1941; ceased publication on the following thirtieth of August.

Toute la France. "Newspaper for those who returned and the families of those still away." Bimonthly, 1941–1944.

La Vie industrielle. Weekly, 1940–1944.

La Vie parisienne. Bimonthly that reappeared "slimmer" on June 10, 1942.

Here are some circulation figures, taken at two different periods: in November, 1940 (from the police records used by M. Langeron in his work, mentioned previously); and in March, 1943 (from statistics established by the head of the Presse-Gruppe, Dr. Eich, at the time of a press exhibition, organized by his services). Note that during the second period, the question of newsprint quotas played an important part.

Paris-Soir easily led all Paris newspapers with a circulation of 970,000 in November, 1940. It dropped to 700,000 in July, 1941, and, after rationing, stabilized at about 300,000 in July, 1942.

Le Petit Parisien recovered many of its readers when it reappeared. In November, 1940, it had a circulation of 680,000. In July, 1942, under a newsprint quota, it kept at 500,000; in other words, it had a circulation of 200,000 over *Paris-Soir* during the same period.

Then came *Le Matin,* with 532,000 in November, 1940. Hit by the quota system, its circulation dropped to 200,000 in July, 1942.

L'Oeuvre took fourth place, with 200,000 in November, 1940. But from July, 1941, onward, its circulation dropped to 100,000. This figure was maintained during the quota period. (In fact, it even rose to 132,000 in March, 1943.)

Aujourd'hui began with a circulation of 100,000, which dropped to 40,000 in July, 1941, and never rose any higher. A parallel case was *Paris-Midi.*

La France au travail, which was specially favored by the German Embassy, started with a circulation of 80,000. In spite of the quota system, it reached 116,000 in March, 1943.

Le Cri du peuple and *Les Nouveaux Temps* benefited from the same artificial support. *Le Cri du peuple* at first sold 35,000 copies, then fell to 20,000 in July, 1941. It rose to 40,000 in July, 1942, and at the peak of the quota system (March, 1943) reached 63,000. *Les Nouveaux Temps* started with a circulation of 20,000, was allotted enough paper for 40,000 in July, 1942, and reached 50,000 in March, 1943.

First place among the weeklies belonged to *Pour Elle* (404,000 copies in November, 1940). *Notre*

Coeur followed it closely with 400,000. After that came the illustrated magazines: *La Semaine* (210,000 copies) and *Tout et tout* (130,000).

La Gerbe sold 135,000 copies, and *Au Pilori*, 90,000. *Paris toujours* and *Vedettes* sold 50,000 each. *L'Atelier* sold 47,000, *La Jeunesse* sold 45,000, and *Le Fait*, 30,000. Finally, the *Journal de la Bourse* and *Camping plein air* each had a circulation of 25,000, but *La Semaine religieuse* and *L'Information universitaire* had a circulation of only 4,500.

NOTES

1. Groussard, *Chemins secrets,* I, 17–18.
2. P. Lazareff, *Dernière Édition* (New York, 1942).
3. Groussard, *op. cit.* pp. 18–21.
4. Conference held at the French Institute in New York on November 19, 1940. Later published in book form as *France Eté 1940* (New York, 1941).
5. Groussard, *op. cit.,* p. 21.
6. E. Dubois, *Paris sans lumière,* pp. 59–60.
7. The word was used by Léon Blum (see his *Mémoires,* pp. 26–30).

8. Colonel Paul Lyet, in his excellent work, *Paris, Open City.* "Revue historique de l'armée" (June, 1948), noted that it was the first time these words were written.
9. Groussard, *op. cit.,* p. 31.
10. Quoted by R. Langeron, *Paris, juin 1940,* p. 38.
11. Groussard, *op. cit.,* pp. 29–30.
12. R. Langeron, *op. cit.,* p. 77.
13. W. L. Shirer, *Berlin Diary* (New York: Alfred A. Knopf, Inc., 1941), p. 43. (Entry for June 18, 1940.)
14. First, General von Vollard-Bockelberg, then General Streccius, and from November 1, 1940, General Otto von Stülpnagel.
15. R. Langeron, *op. cit.,* p. 64.
16. R. Langeron, *op. cit.,* p. 78.
17. R. Langeron, *op. cit.,* p. 99.
18. J. Texcier, *Écrit dans la Nuit,* p. vi–viii.
19. One got into the habit of writing Propaganda-Staffel. The Germans generally used the expression Propaganda-Abteilung.
20. See the report by its head, Dr. Hermann Eich, which was published in 1943 at the time of a French press exhibition (p. 53). A copy of the report, now out of print, is kept in the Bibliothèque nationale.
21. See the article that appeared in *Le Matin* on June 17, 1941.
22. Cf., H. Eich., *op. cit.,* p. 36.
23. Cf., J. Quéval, *Première page, cinquième colonne,* p. 43.
24. For this publication, cf., Quéval, *op. cit.,* pp. 35–41.
25. T. Kernan, *France on Berlin Time* (Philadelphia: J. B. Lippincott Co., 1941), pp. 36–38.
26. Cf., *Le livre d' Or de Paris-Soir,* published in September, 1941, and kept in the Bibliothèque nationale.

It contains many factual details, and numerous photos, showing the very social atmosphere of these functions.

27. Figures given by R. Langeron (*op. cit.*, p. 198) from police headquarters' circulation records. I have compared these figures with the ones given by Dr. H. Eich, for the same period, in his report quoted previously. They correspond perfectly.
28. E. Dubois, *op. cit.*, p. 172.
29. E. Dubois, *op. cit.*, pp. 148–149.
30. An "establishment" in the Saint-Antoine area had this notice on its door: "House closed. Personnel mobilized (*sic*).
31. E. Dubois, *op. cit.*, p. 166.
32. E. Dubois, *op. cit.*, pp. 109–112.
33. E. Dubois, *op. cit.*, p. 166.
34. E. Dubois, *op. cit.*, pp. 124–125.
35. E. Dubois, *op. cit.*, pp. 129–130.
36. And he added: "I quote word for word what he said." Cf., E. Dubois, *op. cit.*, p. 132.
37. There was dancing in Paris during the early weeks of the occupation. The only journalist in the occupied press who found this indecent was, as far as I know, one who worked for *Au Pilori;* on August 2, 1940, he wrote in his paper:

    "In some establishments in the place du Tertre, they are dancing the new—I can only call them 'contortions,' now in fashion. . . . It wouldn't be so bad if the German army weren't watching these antics. In fact, German troops with still and movie cameras take photos of the dancers. They must think the French are in a hurry to forget their defeat."

    Later, dancing was forbidden in public, but dancing lessons were still available. This led to what *La Gerbe* called, on June 11, 1942, "the great dancing-class scandal." Here is what it described:

    "They are held in corridors or yards, in dilapidated places that look like dingy cafés and seedy hotels. . . . You want to join? Nothing easier. You know the address: number so-and-so, such-and-such a street. You go through a large gateway into a yard, which has small workshops on the ground floor, There is an unlit lamp, but in the half-light of a spring evening like this, you can still read the painted letters: 'Dancing class.' . . . In the next room, the manager and his girl assistant sit at a large conference table, piling up the subscriptions and making the accounts tally.

" 'I'd like to . . .'

" 'A hundred francs down and ten francs a night.' " "Swing" at prices to suit all pockets.

38. R. Langeron, *op. cit.,* p. 135.
39. The "French National Party," created at the instigation of the Propaganda-Staffel, under the patronage of *Au Pilori,* comprised two "action groups": the French Guard (young people over twenty-one) and the Young Front (sixteen to twenty-one). Cf., *Au Pilori,* September 30, 1940.
40. T. Kernan, *op. cit.,* pp. 190–191.
41. R. Langeron, *op. cit.,* p. 151.
42. L. Poliakov, *L'etoile jaune,* p. 59.
43. L. Poliakov, *ibid.,* p. 78.
44. L. Poliakov, *ibid.,* pp. 46–47.
45. Report of the twelfth of June quoted by Poliakov in the book cited.
46. Quoted by Poliakov, *ibid.,* pp. 62–63.
47. See my *Histoire du Parti communiste français, 1920–1940,* last chapter.
48. R. Langeron, *op. cit.,* pp. 147–148. An order from the Commander of the Paris Garrison, published the following day, barred the civilian population and Paris police from entering the Bois de Boulogne,

"until further notice" (cf., *Le Matin,* August 14, 1940). This prohibition was lifted after a few days.

49. Quoted by J. Carcopino, then director of the École Normale Supérieure, in his book *Souvenirs de scept ans,* p. 197
50. J. Carcopino, *op. cit.,* p. 123.
51. A mimeographed copy of this collection is kept in the Bibliothèque nationale; cf., p. 37.
52. J. Carcopino, *op. cit.,* p. 216.
53. A. Ouzoulias, *La Vie héroïque du colonel Fabien,* p. 22.
54. Details can be found in A. Ouzoulias' book, quoted above.
55. Rayman was arrested on the sixteenth of November, 1943, Celestino on the seventeeth, and Fontano on the thirteenth.
56. See Colonel Rémy's *Mémoires,* p. 454. It should be noted, however, that the murder of General Schaumberg was, after all, a somewhat different matter from the odd "capture of a rifle."

BIBLIOGRAPHY

ASTIER, E. d'. *Sept jours en été.* Algiers, 1944.

AUDIAT, P. *Paris pendant la guerre. Paris,* 1946.

BARDOUX, J. *La Délivrance de Paris.* Paris, 1945. (Diary of a senator, member of the Institut, from October, 1943 to October, 1944.)

BASALDUA, P. de. *Con los Alemanes en Paris, paginas de un diario.* Buenos Aires, 1943. (Recollections of the years 1940–1941.)

BOURGET, P., and LACRETELLE, C. *Sur les murs de Paris 1940-1944.* Paris, 1959.

BRAIBANT, C. *La Guerre à Paris. Paris,* 1945. (Diary from November 8, 1942 to August 27, 1944.)

CHRISTESCU, D. *Parisul lor.* Bucharest, 1944. (A Rumanian woman's impressions.)

COLETTE. *Paris de ma fenêtre.* Paris, 1944.

CORDAY, P. *J'ai vécu dans Paris occupé.* Montreal, 1943.

DANSETTE, A. *Histoire de la Libération de Paris.* Paris, 1946.

DUBOIS, E. *Paris sans lumière.* Lausanne, 1946.

EICH, H. *Wege der französischen Presse.* Paris, 1943.

EPARVIER, Y. *A Paris, sous la botte des nazis.* Paris 1944. (Collection of photographs.)

EYNARD, P. *Impressions de Paris.* (Paris at the beginning of 1942: impressions of a Swiss. See the Swiss *Le Mois,* April 1942, pp. 81–103.)

FRICAMBAULT, F. de. *Paris, ville occupée.* New Delhi: Publications of the Fighting French Information Bureau, 1943.

FROWEIN, K. *Festung Frankreich fiel.* Berlin, 1940. (See in particular pp. 130–147: "In eroberten Paris, Besuch bei Herrn Reynaud.")

GALTIER BOISSIÈRE, J. *Mon Journal pendant l'occupation.* Paris, 1944.

KENT, V. *Quatre ans à Paris.* Paris 1947.

KERNAN, T. *France on Berlin Time.* Philadelphia: J. B. Lippincott Co., 1941.

KITZING, H. J. *Wir liegen in Paris.* Berlin, 1941.

LAFFARGUE, A. *Le général Dentz, Paris 1940. . . .* Paris, 1954.

LA HIRE, J. de. *Les Horreurs que nous avons vues.* Paris, Tallandier. (Reports which appeared in *Le Matin* during the first two weeks of the occupation.)

LANGERON, R. *Paris, juin 1940.* Paris, 1946.

LINGEMANN, P. *Pariser Tagebuch, 1940.* Berlin, 1941.

MORIENVAL, J. *Films français parus pendant l'occupa-*

tion. Paris, 1945. Published by the Centrale catholique du Cinéma et de la Radio.

MORAWSKI, E. *Der Durchbruch im Westen.* Berlin, 1940. (Day-to-day diary of a German officer.)

PARROT, L. *L'intelligence en guerre. Panorama de la pensée française dans le clandestinité.* Paris, 1946.

POLONSKI, J. *La Presse, la propagande et l'opinion publique sous l'occupation.* Paris, 1946. (Concerned only with the anti-Jewish press and propaganda.)

QUÉVAL, J. *Première page, cinquième colonne.* Paris, 1945.

RAISKY, A. *La presse antiraciste sous l'occupation hitlérienne.* Paris, 1944. (Collection of newspapers, leaflets and proclamations edited by Jewish organizations between the years 1940–1944.)

SCHULZ-WILMERSDORF, P. A. *Paris deutsch geschen.* Berlin, 1941.

VACHER, R. *J'étais à Paris en janvier dernier.* New Delhi: Published by the Fighting French Information Bureau, 1943.

Pages de gloire des vingt-trois. Paris, 1951. (Collective work, dedicated to the memory of Michel Manouchian and his twenty-two companions shot on February 21, 1944.)

La Résistance des intellectuels. New York, 1944. (Mimeographed copy.)

Revue d'Histoire de la Deuxième Guerre Mondiale. Special issue on the French Resistance. July, 1959.

Annuaire de la presse française: 1942–1943. Paris, 1943.

Catalogue des périodiques clandestins en France (1939–1945). (By R. AND P. ROUX-FOUILLET, Paris, *Bibliothèque nationale,* 1954.)